D0607036

HELLO.

01

2006: BE CAREFUL – BIG BROTHER IS WATCHING YOU, BUT...

THE ART OF REBELLION 2

First published 2006 by
Publikat Verlags- und Handels GmbH & Co. KG
Hauptstraße 204
D-63814 Mainaschaff
Tel: +49 (0) 6021 / 90040-0
Fax: +49 (0) 6021 / 90040-20
info@publikat.de

Concept, Art Direction and Design: Christian Hundertmark | C100
email: hello@c100studio.com, http://www.c100studio.com

ISBN: 3-9809909-4-x

Printed and bound in China.

CONTENT

Disclaimer: This book is a documentation of street art as an art movement and urban phenomenon. I don't ask, incite or support anybody to do illegal action, destruction or crime. I'm not responsible for the content of the photos nor any weblink set in the book.

01 George Orwell's Vision. Artists: G, L'Atlas. Paris, FR. 2004
02 Page 006 - 007: "Under Control". Artist: L'Atlas. Paris, FR. 2004

...NO WORRIES,
EVERYTHING'S...

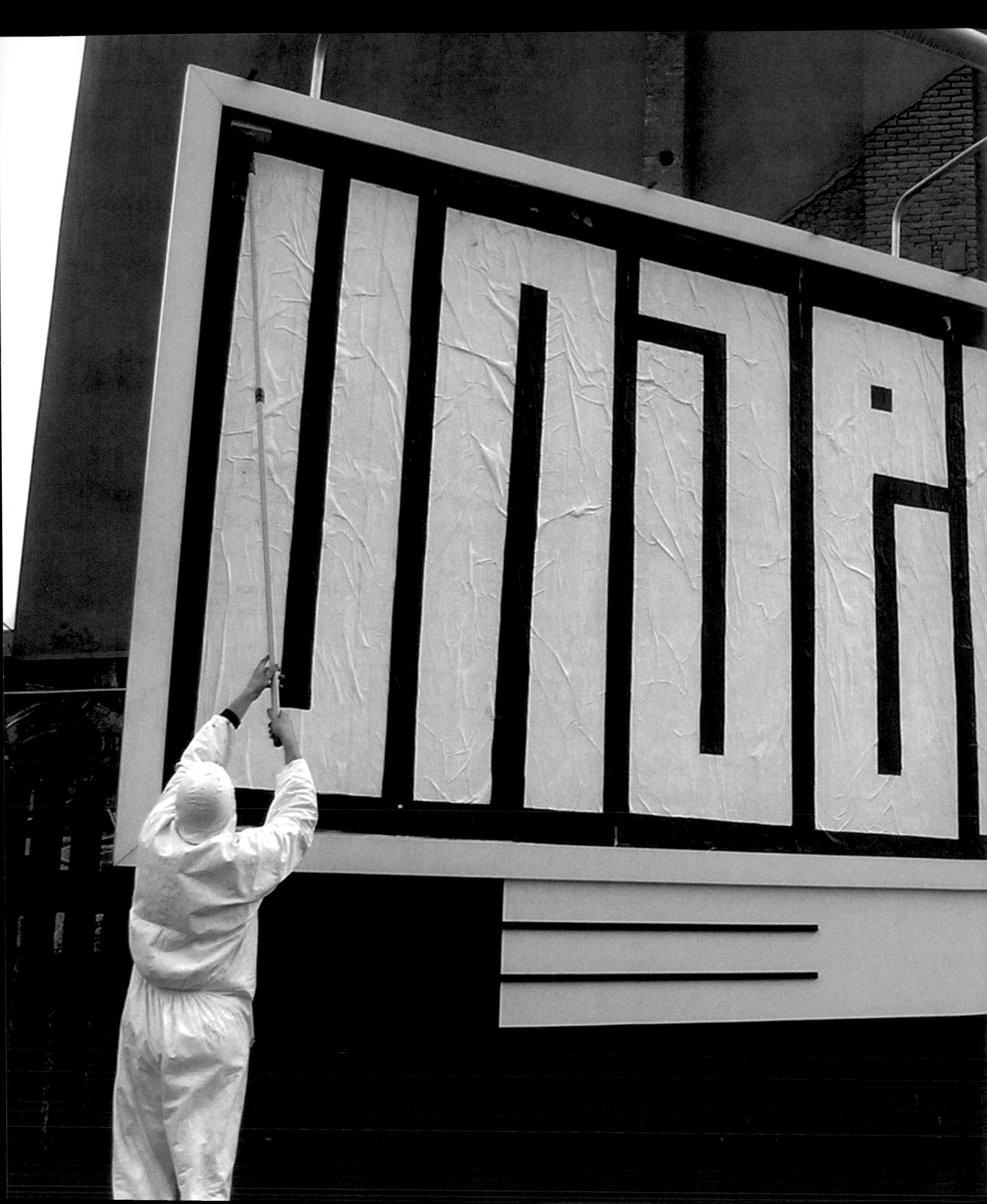

CONTROL
CLEARCHANNEL
More O'Ferrall
BR 513

01

02

03

A lot happened since the my first book "The Art of Rebellion" came out in 2003. Starting with the amazing book release party, where artists from London, New York, Amsterdam, Milan, etc. didn't hesitate to come over to Munich and turned something actually planned as "just a little book release party" into the "Wild Style party of street art" (– Dom from Stickernation.net) by painting the whole area including the toilets, skate decks and cardboards during the day and marker-tattooing numerous girls later that night.

I remember the day after, where we all painted at Munich's hall of fame. I remember all the other artists that slept on my couch since then when they passed Munich on their trips. I remember the couches I slept on in various cities. I remember hanging out with the FK crew and a bunch of other guys on the beach of Barcelona, after enjoying a really amazing "art for free" show the day before. I remember many other great art shows and exhibitions being held all over the world like the Urban Edge in Milan, the Vinyl Killers in San Francisco or the Hollywood remix show the New Yorker Wooster Collective organised. Not to forget the great Asbestos' Secret Santa Swap for christmas – and I also remember my wonderful christmas gift from G*! I remember cycling around Amsterdam at four in the morning with my geezer Galo at Chaz's birthday – when Galo didn't find our way home after a bombing session with Justin Kees. Skin up, Galo! I also remember meeting unexpectedly the New Yorker Faile crew painting a big wall in the red light district. I remember cycling around Stockholm with Akay, helping him and Klisterpete carrying around material from abandonded houses to build a new house on a very steep rock next to the sea. I remember meeting many artists on various occasions in Barcelona, Milan or London and having a great time with them. And I remember receiving gigabytes of emails from artists from all over the world – though it's very difficult to manage replying everyone it's still great to keep in contact!

So many impressions, so many great memories – I could easily fill this page with even more anecdotes but I don't want to bore you with that any longer. What I noticed since I got into street art is, that even if we all live in different countries the worldwide street art scene steady achieves something very special: growing together and exchanging information, which lead to an impressive progression of the whole movement. Thanks to our CNN-like websites Ekosystem.org and Woostercollective.com for keeping everyone updated on a daily basis.

So, welcome to the next level – no worries! Everything's UNDER CONTROL like L'Atlas pasted on a billboard in Paris last year. Street art stepped one step further from just sticker art for "cheap fame" to more conceptual art that is performed in a perfect technical way nowadays. It's amazing to notice a lot of artists starting to actually rethink about what they're creating instead of doing the same thing done a thousand times before. This is what kept me stoked while spending numerous hours of work on this book-project again.

For "Art of Rebellion 1" I asked many artists what they think the future of street art would be: Many feared that it became trendy and being exploited like many other trends before. Luckily the expected boom didn't actually happen that big, though there are newcomers starting almost everyday. Still, there is no reason to complain, even though big companies finally recognised the signs of the times and got into the game, too. Since the bigger part of artists are very conscious of what they do and what they don't want to do, most of them are clever enough to handle this and use it for their own benefit without selling out.

There are projects like i.e. the Fox-hotel in Copenhagen where international artists painted a hotel which proofs that this form of urban art is highly respected nowadays.
There are artists finally getting paid for their work – and they deserve it because they've been working hard on their skills for years. So, it's all good.

On the other hand in times of surveillance cameras and zero tolerance concepts of city councils it got more difficult to get your art to public but still it's not impossible like this book shows. Nowadays street artists just act more clever and use to disguise or work during day time. It's not little kids who do street art, most of them are in their early 30's, it's their life and the refuse to be limited by any rules or laws. They just go for it and they can't be stopped. The same goes for projects like, i.e the Finder Keepers: just doing it – making art for everyone, for free, without paying any rents etc. That's what street art mostly is about from my point of view. Doing your own thing without any limitations, giving something back to the street, making people smile and think, causing reactions. Even if people hate it, at least it caused an reaction and stopped them from being machines in their nine to five jobs.

I know there are people reading this who aren't into this whole urban activism term like me or maybe you – this book is for them to open their eyes! I'm talking to you! Next time you see something that maybe isn't supposed to be there but somehow looks like art, think twice maybe you are the spectator of an artist's new work.
Welcome!
– C100. January, 2006

01 Intervention_F1. Artist: Hietzing station, Vienna, AT. 2005
02 Public urinal. Artist: Influenza. Rotterdam, NL. 2005
03 The pointless oneliner. Artist: Influenza. Hamburg, GER. 2005

01

I will start off this intro with a quote from the late Social Realist, Ben Shahn that reads, "I believe that if it were left to artists to choose their own labels, most would choose none!". Having re-introduced this perception I will comment on the vividly active creative movements that take place around the world in our city streets every day.

For many decades there have been individuals and groups taking their message, and creativity to the city streets to be seen, influenced, criticized, and then re-painted by the public domain. While the message, medium, and tactics vary from person to person what gets called into attention is that we are all creating with persistent passion, and ill-regard to laws and art conformities. I strongly feel that the most courageous, and challenging art form takes place while creating in the streets. In the streets we are able to be anonymous or known, sloppy or clean, witty or angry, or even all at once!

We choose how we want to express ourselves and each outlet holds its own validity. Throw paint on the wall and watch it drip, write your name in Ketchup, or draw a picture with your piss, whatever suits you best at that time, the energy and power comes from within and is acted out in the process of creating. When we work in the streets we work together. To Quote Martin Luther King Jr. "We must learn to live together as brothers or perish together as fools."

Our eyes listen and hear the city streets telling a story to everyone that walks by. In a literal sense the streets have a unity with each other. Each street is woven amongst a large web of energy that forms the city. Respect and acknowledge that each road leads to a different path and each person is able to take a different route to their own destination. The future depends on us at this moment. Do we fall to our own death by criticizing, shutting out, and critiquing other artists and art forms that challenge our own beliefs? Artists and art forms that challenge our perspectives? NO! We need to listen to the walls and appreciate our diversity in the streets. If we fail to admit new ideas, and techniques then we kill the same beauty that encompasses us as artists, that being freedom of expression.

– ABOVE. January, 2006

Just like all art forms, the art on the streets has begun to evolve. Since the first Street art has seen many changes and has been treated as more of a trend then an art form. What was once done with anonymity in the wee hours of the night, is now out in the open and done often in broad daylight. The names are known and even have followings outside the art world. Receiving recognition once again in galleries, what was once strictly in the streets has now been brought inside. Small businesses the world over have employed local "street artists" to liven up their business. From shop front paintings to magazine ad design, how better to give you company the "urban edge" than to employ an artist that works mostly in the streets. Most of these were businesses that supported the art or had some kind of connection; such as record stores, head shops, clothing and shoe stores. But one big down side to the popularity is the fact that it is being used to sell products that have little, to nothing to do with the art. Like any good art/trend the exploitation has also begun. Large businesses have jumped on the "street art" bandwagon and use it regularly to expand their demographic hold.

Last I checked there aren't many street artists driving "Urban" Army Trucks, but their billboard ad campaign reads clearly "Street Art". And then there was the mysterious campaign that almost looked real by a popular video-game company, including stickers, posters and billboard alterations in a mass multi-regional promotional campaign. Neither of these were received too well on the streets by other artists and seemed to backfire in their own way. Although in some cases these gigantic companies used real street artists, they support street art in no way, shape or form and would be the first to vote for stricter laws regarding the art that is produced in the streets. As it is, it seems laws have become a lot stricter the world over. This may have to do with the in your face popularity that street art has received, plus its misused exploitations haven't helped much either. Hopefully the misuse of the art doesn't destroy the realness of the streets. Our art can be taken off the streets, but it should be done with the respect that any art deserves.

– JUSTIN KEES. January, 2006

02

03

01 Artist: Tchin. Toulouse, FR. 2004
02 "Street.art". San Francisco, USA. 2005
03 Campbell soup can. Artist: TV Boy. Barcelona, ESP. 2005

EINDHOVEN
MONED
705

01

WARNING!
choking hazard
DO NOT
BITE!
ARE YOU MAD?
HOW CAN YOU DARE
TO ATTACK ME AFTER
WITNESSING MY
AWESOME POWER?
brrr...
skull
snaps
OLD SKOOL
piece
game ove

02

03

01 Artists: Sol Crew, Space3, The Toasters. Eindhoven, NL. 2005
02 Artist: Jake. London, UK. 2005
03 Artists: DSR Klan. Mexico City, MX. 2004

AVENIR
AUDIEN
AVENIR
MARC
AVENIR
BAR
RESTAURANT
01

02

ADRIAN
03

The CLASH
TO HELL
POCH
04

05

06

07

08

09

10

11

01 Artists: Opt, G, Halieutik. Paris, FR. 2005
02 Artist: Emre. London, UK. 2005
03 Artist: Adrian. Munich, GER. 2005
04 Artist: Poch. Rennes, FR. 2005
05 Artist: Boxi. Berlin, GER. 2005
06 Artist: Tron. London, UK. 2005
07 Artist: Unknown. 2005
08 Artist: Evol. Berlin, GER. 2005
09 Artist: Unknown. 2005
10 Artist: Tower. Berlin, GER. 2005
11 Artist: Unknown. 2005

01

WHAT?
ROCK IS ALIVE!
I WANT HIM DEAD! YOU HEAR ME GOOD?!! KILL HIM!!
mr. Rock

02

03

What me Pervert ?

04

05

06

07

08

01 Artists: Nano 4814, Nuria. Madrid, ES. 2004
02 Artist: Rock. Rennes, FR. 2005
03 Artist: Marxich. Paris, FR. 2005
04 Artist: Draawer. Singapore, SIN. 2005
05 Artist: Chris Silva. Unknown, USA. 2005
06 Artists: Ken, Kode, Freaklub. Barcelona, ES. 2005
07 Artist: Bros. Milan, I. 2005
08 Artists: Kev Grey, Kid Acne, Swain, T-Rex. Sheffield, UK. 2005

01 02 03 04 05 06 07 08 09

10

11

12

13

14

15

16

17

18

THE ART OF REBELLION 2

01 Artist: Nails. Paris, FR. 2005
02 Artist: Jet-Pac. London, UK. 2005
03 Artist: Senor B. Tillburg, NL. 2004
04 Artist: Oles. Rotterdam, NL. 2005
05 Artist: 91111. Munich, GER. 2005
06 Artist: El Euro. Unknown, FR. 2005
07 Artist: 5003. Unknown, USA. 2005
08 Artist: Mr. Fangs. Unknown, USA. 2005
09 Artist: Vinnie Ray. New York, USA. 2005
10 Artist: Unknown. Helsinki, FIN. 2005
11 Artist: Ichi. London, UK. 2005
12 Artist: The Walters. Munich, GER. 2005
13 Artist: Miss Riel. Berlin, GER. 2005
14 Artist: Dave. Los Angeles, USA. 2005
15 Artist: Evil Design. New York, USA. 2005
16 Artist: Foob. Tillburg, NL. 2005
17 Artist: Pure Evil. London, UK. 2005
18 Artist: Sums. Bristol, UK. 2005

01

02

03

04

05

06

07

08

09

10

01 Artist: Tout va Bien. Toulouse, FR. 2005
02 Artist: Klutch. San Francisco, USA. 2005
03 Artist: Hase. Unknown, VE. 2005
04 Artist: Tout va Bien. Toulouse, FR. 2005
05 Artist: Unknown. Vienna, AT. 2004
06 Artist: Unknown. Vienna, AT. 2004
07 Artist: Jose. Munich, GER. 2004
08 Artist: Klutch. San Francisco, USA. 2005
09 Artist: Unknown. Rio de Janeiro, BRA. 2005
10 Artist: 1337. Unknown, USA. 2005

01

02

03

04

05

06

07

08

09

10

01 Artist: Unknown. Munich, GER. 2005
02 Artist: Krooked Seams. Munich, GER. 2005
03 Artist: Mjar. London, UK. 2005
04 Artist: Vincil the Berzerker. Montpellier, FR. 2005
05 Artist: ARRGH!. Hannover, GER. 2005
06 Artist: Akim. Reykjavik, ISL. 2005
07 Artist: Wood. Rotterdam, NL. 2005
08 Artist: 1001. Cologne, GER. 2005
09 Artist: Ariel. Rozumberok, SL. 2005
10 Artist: Cre. French Riviera, FR. 2005

L
U
Z
F
E
A
01

fake
Grüne
rnheim Mitte
Einstieg nur mit gültigem Fahrausweis
Fahrschein-Automat an der Haltestelle
02

E N O R M
03

04

INTERDIT
CÔTÉ IMPAIR
05

06

07

08

09

10

01 Artist: Influenza. Milan, I. 2005
02 Artist: Unknown. Berlin, GER. 2005
03 Artist: Enorm. Frankfurt, GER. 2005
04 Artist: Louise. Brussels, B. 2005
05 Artist: Urban Blooz. Bordeaux, FR. 2005
06 Artist: Deep Inc. Vienna, AT. 2002
07 Artist: Tout va Bien. Toulouse, FR. 2005
08 Artist: Tout va Bien. Toulouse, FR. 2005
09 Artist: ESL. New York, USA. 2005
10 Artist: Hkaestra. Milan, I. 2005

01

02

03

04

05

06

07

08

09

10

11

12

01 Artist: Asbestos. New York, USA. 2005
02 Artist: Rep 1. New York, USA. 2005
03 Artist: Tout va Bien. Toulouse, FR. 2005
04 Artist: Bäst. New York, USA. 2005
05 Artist: Downey. New York, USA. 2005
06 Artist: Rep 1. New York, USA. 2005
07 Artist: Swoon. New York, USA. 2005
08 Artist: Revs. New York, USA. 2005
09 Artist: Al the artist. New York, USA. 2005
10 Artist: Revs. New York, USA. 2005
11 Artist: CKE. Rozumberok, SL. 2005
12 Artist: Espo. New York, USA. 2005

STOCKHOLM
Sweden, 2004

01

02

03

04

05

06

07

08

09

01 Artist: Roket. 2004
02 Deer. Artist: Klisterpete 2004
03 Artist: Unkwon. 2004
04 Artist: Bumble One. 2004
05 Tiger. Artist: Klisterpete. 2004
06 The Barsky brothers building another house. 2004
07 ÜMR. Artist: Unknown. 2004
08 DJ at work. Artist: Unknown. 2004
09 Artist: Unknown. 2004

AMSTERDAM
The Netherlands, 2004

01

02

03

06

04

05

08

09

WIJDESTEEG
CENTRUM

07

THE ART OF REBELLION 2

01 Artist: Fafi (Toulouse, FR). In the red light district. 2004
02 Cat tag. Artist: Unknown. 2004
03 Lamp. Artist: Unknown. 2004
04 Artist: Justin Kees. 2004
05 Artist: TLP, Zevs, Oles. 2004
06 Stickers galore! 2004
07 Artist: Gamebombing. 2004
08 Artist: Unknown. 2004
09 Artist: Waynehorse. 2005

MILAN
Italy, 2005

01

It took a few years to bloom but after a long time of religious dedication to writing Milan's street art scene is now consolidating. Many people start moving into different fields, twisting things up and coming up with more personal and therefor original styles.

The "Urban Edge" show brought together the old and the new skool and all the other shows like "Arteimpropria" or "Now Underground" opened the people's minds a little, inspiring them to experiment more and to feel more easy about bringing something into the street that is not necessarily a tag but something more personal and different. After years of anonymity, Italy and Milan are finally finding their own identity.

A big shout out goes to all the Italian pioneers who brought the culture over and spread it around, implanting the seed of a still growing scene. People like Sean, Kaos, Gruff, Flycat, Shad, Rendo, to name just a few. Other big shouts go out to the Italians who felt the urge to step up into something else before others, like Plank, Luze and Santy and the Krudality Kru, Robot inc. aka 2501, Abbominevole, Ozmo, Pao, 108, Why Style from Rome and of course the undisputed master, my breadren Blu, and my man The Don bringing always good vibes inna place! Respect to y'all! Absolute love to all the newcomers, keep on coming!
– Bo 130. January, 2006

02

03

04

05

06

07

08

09

01 Artist: The Don. 2005
02 Artists: Microbo, Bo130. 2005
03 Bombed wall. 2005
04 Artist: TV Boy. 2005
05 Artist: Bros. 2005
06 Artist: Santy. 2005
07 Artist: Krudality. 2005
08 Artist: Gato. 2005
09 Artist: Gato. 2005

RIO DE JANEIRO
Brasil 2005

01

02

03

04

05

06

07

08

09

01-09 Artists: Unknown. 2005

TLP, BACKJUMPS '06

Berlin, GER

01

01

Artist: The London Police

Location: Berlin, GER. 2005

Comment: Some of my favourite artists live and work in Berlin. It's one of the best places to see graffiti and art in the street. So in August 2005 when the good looking BACKJUMPS team of Adrian, Suze, Hae-lin and Tom invited me to paint the side of 62 Wrangelstraße (Kreuzberg, Berlin) I was happy as larry. My young and enthusiastic volunteer helpers Katherine, Vincent and Erin did basically all the work whilst I skun up a lot in the children's playground below watching groups of gnarly looking geezers get annihilated by midday on big bottles of German beer. Just a couple of streets away are also incredible must-see walls from Huskmithavn and Os Gemeos (also part of the Backjumps project). Together with the ubiquitous Berlin tags and throw ups the neighbourhood is alive and well and I'm just honoured to be in there somewhere.

Comment by Chaz, The London Police. January, 2006

CLOWN NOSE HOUSE

New York, USA

02

02
Artist: Dan Witz
Location: Brooklyn, New York, USA. 2005
Comment: This house front was transformed into a face with the simply add of a red ballon.

WALK
London, UK

01

02

03

04

01-04
Projectname: Walk.
Artist: Constantin Demner
Location: Spitalfields, East London, UK. 2005
Comment: Intervention in public space in East London, UK, using the language of street art to bring local history to life in the imagination of passers-by. Part of Spitalfields has been amended with an information system, allowing the pedestrian to enter a city walk – free of charge, without the need of a tour guide or a guide book, while they go about their daily routine. A 2 km long line has been painted onto the pavement, forming the path to follow between stenciled panels that have also been applied to the pavement, pointing out local history, facts and sometimes more personal associations with the area.
This multidisciplinary intervention makes the bricks and concrete transparent, reawakening interest in the streets and opening people's eyes to the four dimensions through which they move.

Comment by Constantin Demner. January, 2006

SHOPDROPPING

01

02

03

04

01 St. Niklaas, BE. 2005
02 Portland, Maine, USA. 2005
03 Brooklyn, New York, USA. 2005
04 St. Niklaas, BE. 2005

Projectname: Shopdropping
Artist: Ryan Watkins-Hughes
Location: Supermarkets worldwide. 2005
Comment: Shopdropping is an ongoing project in which I change the packaging of canned goods and then "shopdrop" the items back onto grocery store shelves. I replace the packaging with labels created using my photographs. The "shopdropped" works act as a series of art objects that people can purchase from the grocery store. Because the barcodes and price tags are left intact purchasing the cans before they are discovered and removed is possible. In one instance a store employee even restocked the cans to a new aisle based on the barcode information. Shopdropping strives to take back a share of the visual space we encounter on daily basis. Similar to the way "street art" takes a claim to public space for self expression, Shopdropping subverts commercial space for artistic use. The photographs act as a visual journal of my travels over the past few years. Displayed in nonlinear combinations the images remix the traditional narrative of the passing of time. The vibrant individuality of each image is a stark contrast to the repetitive, functional, package design that is replaced.

Comment by Ryan Watkins-Hughes. January, 2006

HOMELESS
New York, USA

01

01
Location: New York, USA. 2000
Comment: During my first trip to NYC, in September 2000, I was searching for urban pieces that I could "shadow" following the work I started in Paris two years prior. I had actually found and "flashed" quite a few subjects. There was one single idea that had captivated my attention and desire but I could not bring myself do. Maybe, it was because of the emotional, political and graphical strength that it evoked within me. All of these reasons made me take some time before I could go into action. It was the image and the simple reality of a homeless man sleeping under a street lamp with his shopping cart filled with all of his worldly possessions. All of this man's life in a shopping cart, nothing more, lighted by a NYC street lamp. An exhibition for all of us to see. I watched him for the course of the day. During the day this man was away hunting and gathering within the city as night fell he would find his place to sleep on the street. I finally got up the courage to "shadow" him one night while he was asleep. I was creating a new piece of work but, at the same time, homage to a man which the world has forgotten, becoming real as I decided to mark his absence. His absence became his eternal presence.

Comment by Zevs. January 2006

We apologise for the bad photo quality but we thought it should be included due to the impact of the whole action and the story behind it.

PLATTENBAU

Berlin, GER

02

02
Artist: Evol
Location: Berlin, GER. 2005
Comment: The affixed windows transform this electricity box into a typical East German tower block (German slang word therefor is Plattenbau).

THE UNPLUGGED DEER

Arlon, BE

01

01

Artist: The Plug

Location: Arlon, BE. 2005

Comment: This deer is the symbol of my hometown Arlon. I was stunned that people love a "vulgar" piece of meat instead of honoring people who help our society progress like e.g. doctors. So I had to transform this symbol into a vulgar pack of meal including label (with the accomplice of Mlle Jeanne). You are the meat of society... unplug the system! The deer stayed 5 days like that.

Comment by The Plug. October, 2005

GOT FIRE?
Munich, GER

02

02
Artist: Anonymous
Location: Munich, GER. 2004
Comment: These rolls of hay have been a great invitation to do some mischef with them. What about transforming them into a huge cigarette? Caused great confusion among passers-by.

INVISIBLE GRAFFITI

Paris, FR

01

01
Location: Paris, FR. 2006
Comment: The visible is ephemeral–the invisible is eternal.
Graffiti is made in the nighttime to see the light of day. That is the aim. But not always the result.
Nowadays graffiti is written as quickly as it is erased. Nowadays, when the sole word graffiti is pronounced to be denounced, when simply selling bombs to minors has been forbidden in Great Britain and New York, when the conditions under which graffiti is made are more and more demanding, writers are forced to reconsider the premises of graffiti to make graffiti.
In Paris, after the tag became omnipresent in the 90's, after the great cleaning of the city in 1999, graffiti has entered a new phase with a new generation of writers making so-called post-graffiti or street art. Artists which respond to the situation of today. But one of them, Zevs, will no longer merely adjust himself to these conditions. With a new strategy, Invisible Graffiti, he sets out to change them.
But what is Invisible Graffiti, if not an oxymoron? Is it not two words which do not go together?
Graffiti is made to be seen. Graffiti which cannot be seen cannot be graffiti. But neither is it graffiti when erased. Bombing the city with invisible ink Zevs' graffiti does not see the day of light. In the daytime when the cleaners go out to clean off the tags, there is nothing there. But in the nighttime, when the city is lit up, because the sun goes down, Zevs' graffiti makes its appearance on city walls. It is the city which brings it to light.
Zevs is not just changing his techinical means, replacing paint with ink. He is also changing the conditions, which dictate his means to an end, i.e. graffiti as always. By replacing the neon tubes with flouroscent tubes Zevs litterally sheds a new light on graffiti. A light which makes appear his invisible graffiti, that which is normally not there.
Under the guidance of Zevs, the city enacts what it denounces. Graffiti is no longer made in the nighttime to see the light of day. Invisible Graffiti sees the light of day to be seen at night – the result being no different than the aim.

Comment by Toke Lykkeberg. January, 2006

WWW.ZEVS.FR.ST

DC GECKO

Unknown, FR

01

02

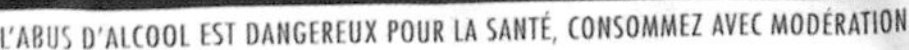

03

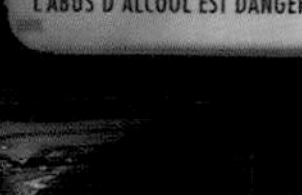

04

01-04
Location: Unkown, FR. 2005
Comment: DC Gecko's unique project of "hacking" advertising boxes plays very impressively with the daytime/nighttime aspects of street art. During the day people aren't able to discover the artwork, only at night, when the lightboxes are switched on, you can see DC Gecko's work. Furthermore there is a link between his name "DC Gecko" and the name of the firm that installs the shelters for the ads "JC Decaux".

ABOVE'S EUROPE TOUR

In Summer 2005 San Francisco-based artist Above left his marks in almost every european country. Here are some stories he experienced:

01

02

Copenhagen
Location: Copenhagen, DK. 2005
Comment: Sometimes I get concerned about my judgment calls!! After hours on top of hours of painting this piece I wanted to have a clean photo with the whole piece in a single frame. PLAN A: The idea was to stay dry and have a passing boat let me on to its deck and then take a photo from there while never getting wet. Wishful thinking! PLAN B: The idea was to swim out in the water while holding my camera above sea level, take the photo and then come back to the dock with the photo and a dry camera. I was left between a rock and a hard place. I decided to go ahead with Plan B and started stripping down into my shorts getting ready for the swim out into the cold salt water. I get into the water and swim about 20 feet out, I turn around and I'm still too close to fit the ABOVE piece into my camera frame, I swim what seems like 60 feet farther with only my right arm in the air holding the camera dry, while my left arm is paddling like a speedboat in the water keeping me from drowning. I freaked out and I just started to point the camera at the distant wall and hope that something came out in the end. A new „PLAN C" starts to enter my head. I'm some 80 feet out from the dock and am really getting tired swimming with just 1 arm. PLAN C: was if I was starting to drown to drop the camera in the water and save my life hoping that even then I could make it back to the dock. "Simple Ideas, Stubbornly Pursued" I think to myself. Plan B was growing tired but still had some energy in it before I aborted everything and tried to save my life from drowning. Some fear endorphins and second wind kicked in and helped me swim back to the dock. Was the photo worth all the effort...? I'll let you make that decision.

Brussels
Location: Brussels, BE. 2005
Comment: It is crazy and strange how things manifest sometimes. I was walking by this house and noticed in the window a variety of wood cabinets, and furniture that attracted my eye. The owner saw me looking in the window at his work and came outside to talk with me. The owner of the house I later came to find out was a cabinet maker and made his money selling his wooden creations. He asked if I did wood work? Well sort of... I make wooden arrows. I drew a picture of one of the arrows but he didn't really understand. I mentioned to him that I also paint arrows on buildings and walls. I showed him some images on my camera of work I had just done in London the week prior and before you know it one thing led to another and the next day I was painting the whole side of his house with arrows! It's a funny and exciting world we live in.

03

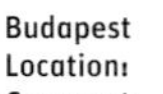

Budapest
Location: Budapest, HU. 2005
Comment: Let me start off by saying that it's a mysterious world we live in! Everyday, life is filled with random possibilities and outcomes. I took a train from Vienna to Budapest with a friend of mine named Killion. Later on that night we were going to meet up with a friend of Killion's who was letting us stay at his apartment while we were in Budapest. Before meeting with Killion's friend, we did some sight seeing of Budapest atop the St. Peters Church's touristy Viewpoint. Once on top of the Church's roof I was searching the skyline for possible rooftops to paint. Sure enough there was one large roof that stuck out from all the others. I made a mental note of the rooftop's location and we left to see more sights. Later, on our way back to meet up with our friend at his apartment he mentioned that access to his building was difficult because there was a gun fight scene being filmed in his staircase for an upcoming Steven Spielberg film called MUNICH. Security was extremely tight to get in to his building for obvious reasons. Our friend came down and let us inside and we climbed several stories of stairs until getting to his apartment. Killion and I ask if there was access to the roof of the building so we could see the city and perhaps other rooftops to paint. Our friend gave us the keys to unlock the top door and showed us the way to the roof. As we get up to the roof and outside we soon realize that this is the same roof we saw from the St.Peters Church viewpoint. For several moments I couldn't believe the situation and sheer luck of being able to have access to the fresh, large wall. The next day Killion and I went to the paint store and stocked up on gallons of latex paint, rollers, and extensions for painting the wall later that night. It was the afternoon when we returned from the paint store back to the building.
We had to wait outside for over an hour as Steven Spielberg was filming a scene. After the scene was shot we were granted entry. This is where the crazy gets crazier! Imagine us carrying up the stairs two large roller extensions, gallons of latex paint, and an array of other painting supplies among Hollywood camera's and actors. As we get closer to the hallway we are stopped as Steven Spielberg himself is acting out a future scene's roll for the characters of the movie. We wait until he is finished and walk by him with all our paint supplies. We were both shocked at the abnormal turn of events. However there was an obvious negative side to this encounter, that being the fact that everyone, including the security guards saw us with painting supplies. If they were to put 2 and 2 together they could easily know that we were responsible for the fresh paint on the side of the building that would take place later that night! I made the final call and decided that the situation was too good to pass up despite the obvious fact that I could get identified and busted even after painting the wall. Later that night we got on top of the roof and I started to paint the wall. I was hanging upside down while Killion was watching the street below for any people that might see me painting. I was 2 letters into the roller piece when a neighbor across the street on the 4th floor was out on his balcony smoking a cigarette and saw me hanging down painting on the roof. Not taking any further chances of getting busted I had to finish the piece in a quick and sloppy manner. These letters and their style are shitty and sloppy, yet better to have made a mark than nothing at all. We packed our supplies quickly and hid in our friend's house until morning. The next day we took photos then left Budapest for Germany with smiles on our faces.

04

Vienna
Location: Vienna, AT. 2005
Comment: Seize the moment, right?! I saw these shutters the first night I was in Vienna. The next day I returned to the shutters to feel out the situation. The location, size, and visibility of these shutters were all on point I went back to the youth hostel and got my paint, then returned and started painting. The hardest part about doing a daytime illegal is convincing the public that you are "suppose" to be painting on the wall. Doing a lot of detail on an illegal is convincing to the public viewer, and police that the painting is legitimate. After about an hour of painting sure enough the police arrive. Two angry cops get out of the car and start yelling at me in German. I tell them I speak English and they demand an explanation for the paint on the wall in addition to verifying my passport. I already had a story fabricated and kept telling it to them over and over. In order to call and talk with the owner of the shutters to see if in fact I did have permission as I told them they needed the address of the building. The funny thing was it took the two cops about twenty minutes to locate the address that was eventually found on the rear side of the building. They started making phone calls (I assume to the owner?) one after the other with no luck of reaching anyone. Despite our spoken language barrier, I could easily understand the frustration of these two cops in their body language. As time grew so did their lack of patience. The two cops confiscated my paint while we waited for a phone call from either the police headquarters or the owner, I'm still unsure. Either way they got the call on the phone, and told me they reached the owner and he said I didn't talk with him and that it was "not O.K." to paint on his wall. Thinking I'm taking a ride to police headquarters in a few minutes the cops surprised me with handing me back my passport and saying that "this is not the United States and that I can't paint other people property in Austria." I wanted to finish the painting but didn't want to push my luck by asking for my cans back, or if I could finish. On the walk back to the youth hostel I couldn't help but wonder if the Austrian police thought that painting on other peoples property in the USA was actually legal?!

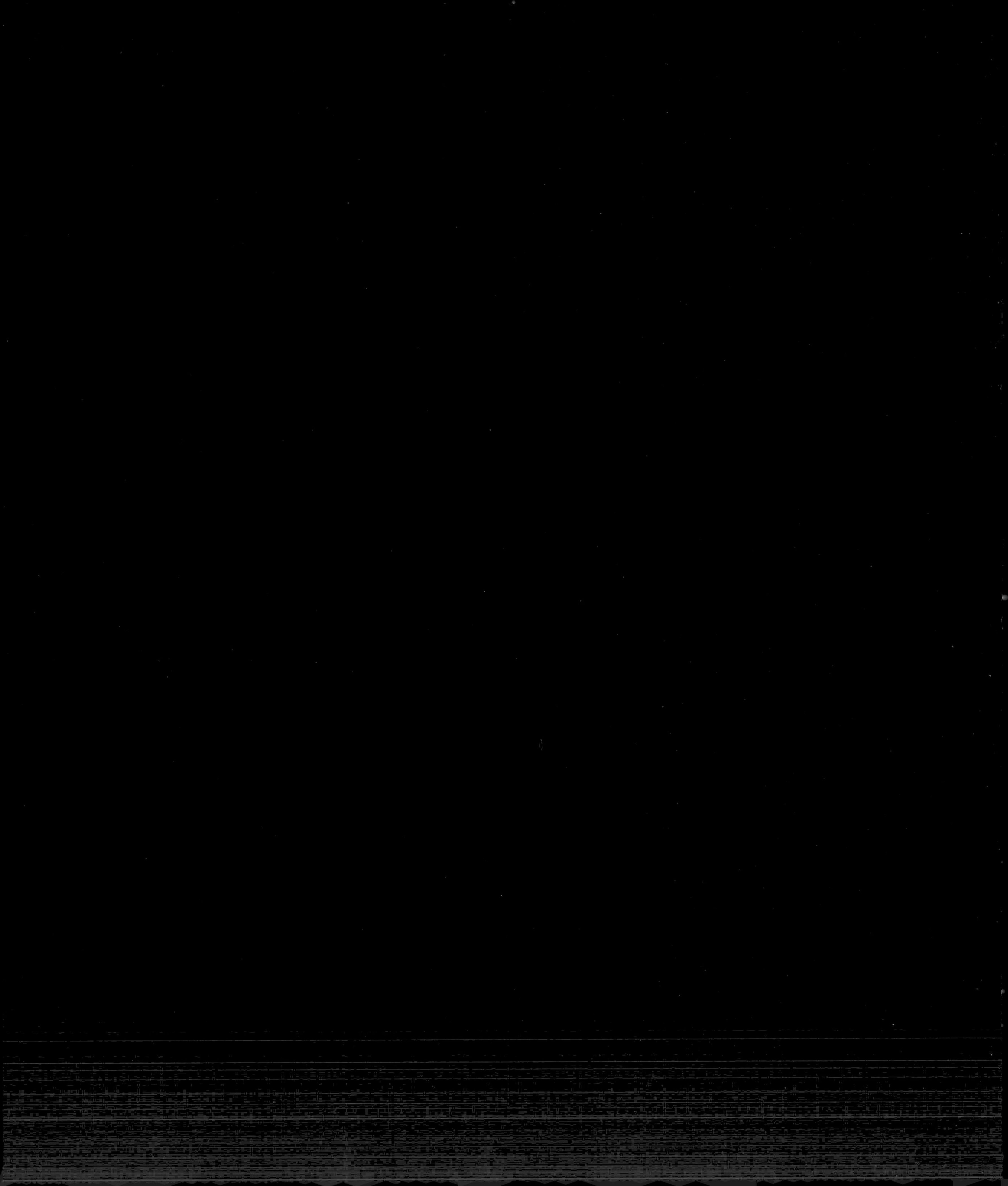

ARTISTS' PROFILES

BLEK LE RAT

Paris, FR

01

If we are art soldiers, then Blek is the Don Corleone. So why is he so important? He is the first stencil artist to produce lifesize figures on the streets, and to inspire others with his prolific politically charged international output. Monochrome images of soldiers appear placed at Checkpoint Charlie in Berlin, Neo Classical nudes appear like angels in derelict Chateaus outside Paris and Arabic figures lurk around corners in Morocco. Blek pioneered stencil graffiti art, introducing the technique into graffiti in Paris in 1981 and has widely influenced probably every stencil artist EVERYWHERE because he is so darn good. It's Blek's world, but you are welcome to play in it...
– Pure Evil. January, 2006

WWW.BLEKLERAT.TK

02

03

04

01 Soldier. Checkpoint Charlie. Berlin, GER. 2003
02 Napoleon fucks sheeps. Paris, FR. 2004
03 Marrakesh, MA. 1989
04 Paris, FR. 1989

01

02

THE ART OF REBELLION 2

An Interview with Blek Le Rat
Name: Blek Le Rat **Age:** 54 **Hometown:** Paris, FR
Cities where to find your art?
Paris, Buenos Aires, Prague, Leipzig, Berlin, London, Taipei, New York, Barcelona, Toledo, Florence, Marokko, Neapel, Wiesbaden, Cologne, Faro.
How did you come up with yor style, do you have a special message?
My first stencils were little black rats, that I spraypainted as if they were running along the streets of Paris during winter 1981. I painted many of them.
In the beginning of the eighties an American artist called Richard Hambleton came to Paris. He was the first artist in public space to export his art and he inspired me to create and spraypaint bigger, life-sized figures. Another source of inspiration was the film "The bigger splash" by David Hockney, which I watched in the seventies and in which Hockney can be seen painting a lifesized man on the walls of an appartment. Since long I don't have a message any more that equals a cry for hate, rebellion or violence. Contrary to a great number of public artists whose exclusive artistic way of expressing themselves is with messages like "Fuck the police", "Fuck the Queen", "Fuck pigs" or "Fuck the government". For they know very well that this kind of messages is appreciated by many. My message is more an educative one. I'm more interested in showing the world that urban art is more than just art of rebellion, but an artform that speaks about poetry and everyday life and is a reflection of our society. Luckily there are other artists like Swoon in the US for example who begin to develop other concepts.
How did you get into street art?
I started in 1981 in Paris with urban art, because I had seen the first graffities on a journey to New York ten years earlier. I introduced stencils to urban art, because I didn't want to spray pieces or tags in Paris. I thought that neither the French architecture nor the French culture were suited to that, because they had no connection to the American. And it would have been totally anachronistic for me to spray tags in Paris in 1981. I used the old stencil-technique to spraypaint rats because as a kid on a journey to Padua in Italy had seen a stencil that showed Mussolini and was a relict of WW II. Beginning with little rats I soon honed my skills to spray big characters two years later. Already in 1981 I was aware of the dimensions of streetart and wanted to be a part of it.

Your favorite street artists:
Gérard Zloytykamien because of his artistic integrity. Swoon because of not doing the same that all the others are doing.
Other interests:
Nothing but my art.
How does a typical day in your life look like?
I lead a normal family life, with all its duties and responsibilities with the only difference that I don't go to work in the morning but travel on a regular basis.
Do you have any stories related to street art?
That would be too long of a story, because it's the story of my life (for 25 years) with all its highs and downs. The last anecdote is from Taipei, November 2005. The day of the vernissage of my exhibition I got to know the minister of tourism and we talked for a long time. At the end of our conversation he told me that I could count on him whenever I would get in trouble caused by graffiti. That never happened to me before and his words were like a ticket to freedom for me.
What do you think is the future of street art, how did it change in the past few years in your opinion?
I think there are many nice days for street art to come. Despite of this movement existing for more than 35 years now it is only at the beginning of its evolution. Luckily the big American wave has lost some of its power, what gives artists world-wide the opportunity to express themselves individually with different techniques. China is a country with relatively few graffiti. And I'm curious to see how Chinese artists adopt this kind of art and develop it with their means and their sensitivity.
Five things you couldn't live without and why:
1. News because the are my brain food.
2. Communication, for me it's like a therapy.
3. Chinese Philosophy (Yi King), the world's oldest book, which allows us to have a look into our fate.
4. Art because it's my life.
Things you don't like:
Tourist attractions, the feeling of being slave to my life, relationships in daily life that are similar to slavery, misunderstandings.

03

01 London, UK. 2004
02 Centaur. Paris, FR 2004
03 Beggars. Paris, FR. 2004

URBAN BLOOZ

Bordeaux, FR

01

Urban Blooz is an art project which started in 2003. It is a reaction to the colonization of public spaces by advertisement. The content of the billboards is getting erased and replaced by a poster showing the frame of the enviroment, that is covered by the billboard itself. This creates a game/play between the pedestrians and the urban enviroment. It is also about a reflection of the usage and function of graphism.

HTTP://URBLOOZ.FREE.FR

02

03

04

05

01 Poster on billboard. Bordeaux, FR. 2004
02 Poster on billboard. Bordeaux, FR. 2004
03 Poster on billboard. Bordeaux, FR. 2004
04 Poster on billboard. Bordeaux, FR. 2004
05 Poster on billboard. Bordeaux, FR. 2004

KID ACNE

Sheffield, UK

01

Sheffield-based Kid Acne began painting graffiti in the early 1990's after a friend showed him Subway Art and Spraypaint Art. They "did a painting that weekend and went tagging with the left overs". His current style and the idea of painting an alternative to B-Boys was inspired by writers such as She One and Fire DFM and the illustrations of Tom Barwick and Pete Fowler around 1995.

"There is no real message as such, just the exploration of composition, the characters interaction and the idea of graffiti as folklore" he says. His work has been exhibited in many galleries throughout Europe, America and Australia. He has also provided illustrations for brands such as Prada (I) and Sixpak (F) as well as prominent British labels Fenchurch, Big Dada, Warp and Lex.

Besides doing groundbreaking art, Kid Acne enjoys kissing girls, playing records, making music and eating cooked dead animals of the BBQ.

WWW.KIDACNE.COM

02

01 Spraypaint. Sheffield, UK. 2005
02 Kid Acne, Kev Grey & Dixie. Spraypaint. Sheffield, UK. 2005
03 Poster. Sheffield, UK. 2005
04 Poster. Sheffield, UK. 2005
05 Poster. Sheffield, UK. 2005

03

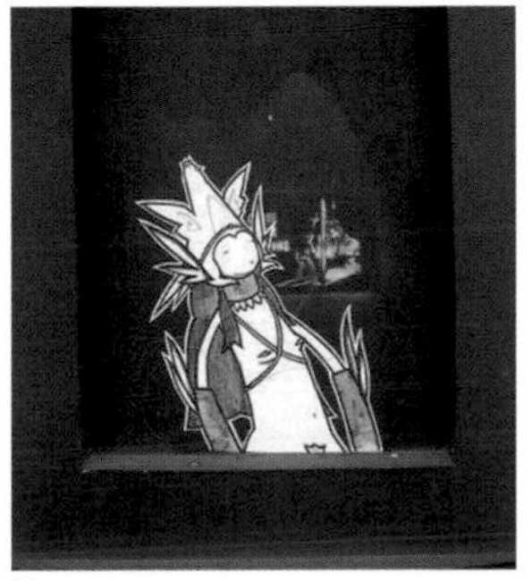

04

05

DOMA

Buenos Aires, ARG

01

DOMA is a group of Argentines that started in the Buenos Aires street art scene in 1998 doing urban installations, stencils, street-projections and absurd campaigns. They studied illustration, film and graphic design. Since the beginning they started creating conceptual universes, different worlds and characters that have been evolving to come alive later with the group's specialization in animation, motion graphics, filming, VJing and toy design. The Argentine reality from the third world has shaped DOMA's productions since the beginning. The main example of this is the "Roni Project". In 2003 after the Argentine Crisis, Doma came out with a crazy and absurd President Campaign of a character called Roni, a parody of Ronald McDonald.

"Understanding the world as a big lab helps to detect the reaction to each action. We are living in a special moment in history. This scenario calls for action. DOMA tries to interfere in all information channels available. Working with the same elements as them, with a bit of irony... thus sparking change in people's perception; offering another point of view. The process: Cross ideas. Action–Reaction."
– DOMA. January, 2006

02

03

04

05

06

07

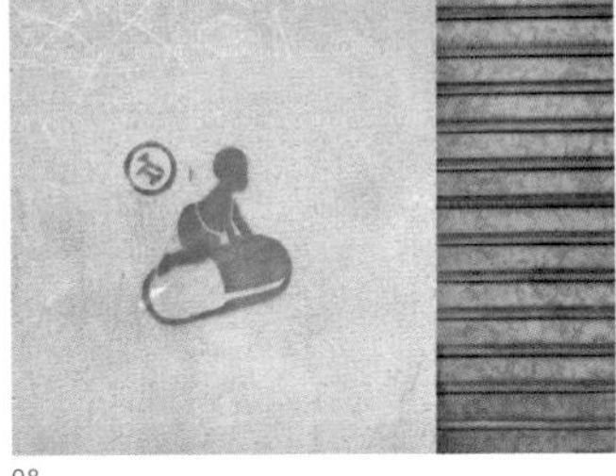

08

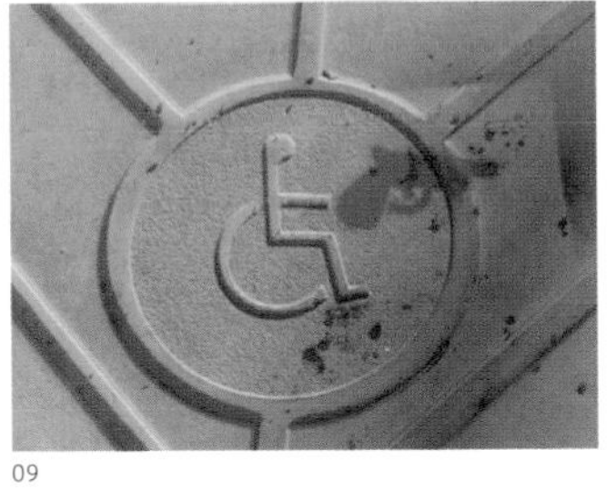

09

10

01
Location: Calle Florida, Buenos Aires, ARG. 2005
Comment: Our extra large stuffed dummy represents a victim of the Argentine Crisis. He is lying dead at an important bank entrance. Was really funny how after this photo, a group of poor kids that where asking for money at the Buenos Aires Downtown, started playing with him jumping over his belly.

02
Location: Barcelona, ES. 2003
Comment: In 2003 we were invited to a conference in this city and at night we went out with a group of local street artists to do some pieces. We did a bunch of stencils from the Roni Campaign.

03
Location: Barcelona, ES. 2003
Comment: The Poster from the Roni Campaign.

04
Location: Barcelona, ES. 2003
Comment: We love cones!

05
Location: Buenos Aires, ARG. 1998
Comment: This is the first thing we did on the streets in 1998. With the same concept of playing with instructional iconography we printed these bands in silkscreen and then glued them onto trashcans.

06
Location: Buenos Aires, ARG. 1999
Comment: This is a crowded street were people use to cross like cattle.

07
Location: Buenos Aires, ARG. 2000
Comment: Our logo stenciled at a playground in a park. Conceptualy this is funny because DOMA means rodeo in spanish, and this game is like a bull, that you have to ride.

08
Location: Barcelona, ES. 2003
Comment: Another stencil from the Roni Campaign. Taking this concept to Europe. Kids in Roni World.

09
Location: Buenos Aires, ARG. 1999
Comment: This stencil is part of the first series we did in 1999. At this time we were obsessed with the action of interfering signals and information channels with the same elements. In this case the result is pretty strong.

10
Location: Buenos Aires, ARG. 2005
Comment: Quick freehand Character, that one of us has drawn all over the city in 2005.

Comments by DOMA. November, 2005

JON BURGERMAN

Nottingham, UK

01

02

03

04

Jon Burgerman is a UK-based artist, known for his doodling, drawing, scrawling and illustration. Jon started spreading his doodles and strange creations out on to walls, lampposts and cash machines around the UK in 2001. His work often features maniacally charged characters, vibrantly coloured and sometimes intertwined. They have become instantly recognisable across the many platforms in which he works, which includes paintings, drawings, textiles, animation and recently 3D vinyl and plush toys.

WWW.JONBURGERMAN.COM

05

THE ART OF REBELLION 2

NAME: Jon burgerMan AGE: 26 HOMETOWN: NoHingham, UK

CITIES WHERE TO FIND YOUR ART: NoHingham, London → various UK cities plus various other places

HOW DID YOU COME UP WITH YOUR CHARACTER/STYLE? Laziness

DO YOU HAVE A SPECIAL MESSAGE?

R

HOW DID YOU GET INTO STREETART AND WHY?

Mistake, but a happy one

FAVORITE STREETARTISTS & WHY:

Kao-alexone – Chimp – Freakclub - Kid Acne - Adam Neate + lots more

OTHER INTERESTS:

eating crisps

HOW DOES A TYPICAL DAY IN YOUR LIFE LOOK LIKE? →

INSPIRATIONS:

books, nooks + crooks

YOUR FAVORITE MUSIC:

DO YOU HAVE ANY STORIES RELATING TO STREETART?

SPRAY IT

DON'T

SAY IT

WHAT DO YOU THINK IS THE FUTURE OF STREETART?

HOW DID IT CHANGE IN THE PAST FEW YEARS IN YOUR OPINION?

More of everything

5 THINGS YOU COULDN'T LIVE WITHOUT AND WHY?

1. tea
2. cake
3. stickers
4. Pens, biro's, markers, felts, crayons, Pencils, paints + Poscas
5. more tea.

THINGS YOU DON'T LIKE:

Angry dogs, Neo-cons, the man, Waste cars, Wars, guns, stale cake, celery cold tea

ANY ADVISE / LAST WORDS?

keep on doodling

06

07

THE ART OF REBELLION 2

01-04 Stickers. Nottingham, UK. 2005
05 DJ booth. London, UK. 2005
06 Dream Bags Jaguar Shoes. London, UK. 2004
07 Plank. Nottingham, UK. 2005

ELPUSSYCAT

Rotterdam, NL

01

Rotterdam-based artist ElPussycat takes street art to a new level by using the simple technique of a camera's time exposure and a blazing flashlight. His motives are mostly cats, snails and characters well-integrated into the ambience. ElPussycat exhibited his work in in New York in 2005.

WWW.FOTOLOG.NET/ELPUSSYCAT

02

03

04

05

01 Skateboarder in half pipe. Rotterdam, NL. 2005
02 Construction worker. Rotterdam, NL. 2005
03 Cat. Rotterdam, NL. 2005
04 Snail. Rotterdam, NL. 2005
05 Drunk guy. Rotterdam, NL. 2005

YOK
Perth, AU

01

d raised in Perth, Australia on beer and barbecue's. goyles. In medieval times gargoyles were placed on from this thought Yok puts his art on city walls to roof tops visible from the streets below to display

ne, Sydney, Perth, Tokyo, New York, Bangkok,

65

WWW.THEYOK.COM

02

03

04

05

01 Poster. Perth, AU. 2005
02 Poster. Perth, AU. 2005
03 Poster. Perth, AU. 2005
04 Poster. Perth, AU. 2005
05 Installation. Perth, AU. 2005

BLU

Bologna, I

01

02

Blu started out his artistic career without a well-defined artistic project, following his passion for drawings, public art and particularly unauthorized illegal art. His work originates from hundred of sketches jotted down in his sketchbook which also represents a diary as a training exercise for the actual work: the mural. With a insane passion for big walls, he's continuously searching for the perfect building to be covered with his surrealistic strong figures. He stopped using spraycans a while ago and now uses the most traditional and essential painting tools: brushes, paint roller, one colour and black. He often uses techniques from scenography like working with long sticks, which simplifies working on bigger walls. Inspiration stems from the need of creating and sharing his art with people to sheer pleasure of transforming ordinary and decaying places; showing how creativity may redevelop from urban degradation.

WWW.BLUBLU.ORG

01
Location: Bologna, I. 2005
Comment: This is the biggest piece I've done so far and one of the few authorized project i've ever done. The cities mayor has never loved the idea and still wants to clean it but it's too expensive.

02
Location: Managua, NIC. 2005
Comment: This piece is part of a mural project called "murales de octubre", a public art festival in Managua (Nicaragua). We were invited there for confronting our muralism with the great muralism tradition of central america. This was a great experience. There were very nice people and very good artists there.

DIST

Colchester, UK

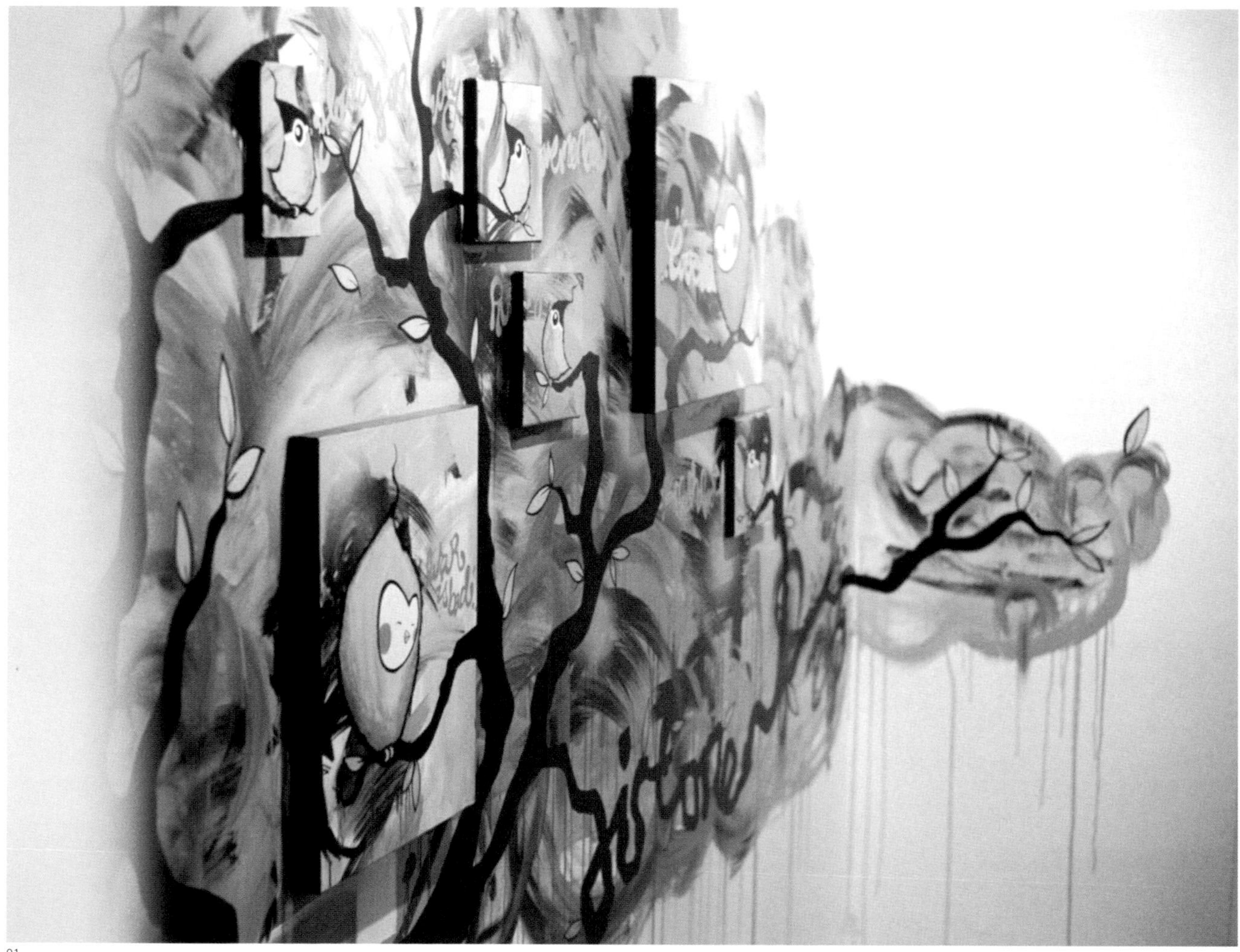

01

Tired of his characters existing only in sketch books and unfinished comics David Earl Dixon chose to take to the streets as alter ego Dist.One in order to bring to life his enigmatic characters and words. An artist of stillness and distance, Dist.One continues to permeate his surroundings with his desires as an artist, as well as exhibiting collections, installations and pieces when situations present themselves.

A world humbly created from the strange to the surreal, haphazardly drawing inspiration from skateboarding, punk rock, comic books, nature and the realms of children's fantasy. Dist urges you to keep an eye on what's around you, it may be changing underneath your nose.

WWW.DISTONE.CO.UK

02

03

04

05

06

01 Woodsman. Colchester, UK. 2005
02 Japanese lady. Colchester, UK. 2005
03 Unlocked pathways. Hand painted then ridden skateboard. Colchester, UK. 2005
04 "I am lost" Installation. Colchester, UK. 2005
05 Laughing Magician. Wheat paste. Colchester, UK. 2005
06 Feldman the b.boy. Wheat paste. Colchester, UK. 2005

ROADSWORTH

MontreaL, CAN

01

Roadsworth started stenciling images onto Montreal streets shortly after 9/11. His first symbol was the cyclist's symbol painted on the street placing it at various points in the city, so it seemed as a visual proposal for more bike paths. "Since almost 90% of concrete in cities is only allowed for cars, which produce traffic and congestion, that continues unchecked, and relentlessly cause pollution, cyclists and pedestrians are not given much of a share in the public space" he says. His work can be seen as a logical reaction to this fact.

Surprisingly many people who see his art in public think it has been done by the city. Unfortunately, still there is a criminal attitude against his art: In November 2004 he was caught by the police and is currently facing criminal charges and a possible fine of 265.000 Canadian dollars for breach of public security.

02

03

04

01 Zipper. Montreal, CAN. 2004
02 Shoeprint. Montreal, CAN. 2004
03 Speakers. Montreal, CAN. 2004
04 Birthday candles. Montreal, CAN. 2004

01

An Interview with Roadsworth

Name: Roadsworth **Age:** 31 **Hometown:** Montreal, CAN

Cities where to find your art?
Montreal, Barcelona, Normandy.

How did you come up with yor style, do you have a special message?
Inspired by the work of Andy Goldsworthy, street signage and high contrastillustration in general. Style is the result of my relatively limited technical ability and the desire to superimpose a relatively large image onto an even larger surface as quickly and efficiently as possible. My main message is: ride your bike.

How did you get into street art?
I got into it through friends that were into it at one time or another. I also wanted to be the urban version of Andy Goldsworthy. Or at least my idea of what that might be. I also wanted to see more bike paths in the city which is why my first stencil was that of a bicycle.

Your favorite street artists:
Glenn Lemesurier, a local cat (Montreal), that takes over vacant lots with his wacky sculptures making condo developers think twice. Other locals, like, Other cause he's got a unique flavour. Akim from Berlin, cause his shit is off the hook. Atlas, cause his work is not only highly original but one of his weather veins or whatever you call them helped me orient myself in Paris once, when I was lost. Ron English, cause he's a pioneer and a subversive. Francisco Garcia, cause he's got the same birthday as me and he turns everyday people (friends, family) into poster boys/girls the way it should be.

Other interests:
Playing keyboards, yoga, movies, dancing.

How does a typical day in your life look like?
Starts with a coffee or two followed by a lot of running around.

Inspirations:
Right now, Barcelona (just got back), music and of course lovely ladies.

Your favorite music:
Music, that makes me want to dance.

Do you have any stories related to street art?
Just stories of getting busted and getting hit on by gay guys. Sometimes I wonder, if one of the cops, that busted me wasn't a little too thorough with his frisking. I'm not homophobic or anything, but I have a pretty good gaydar (gay radar).

What do you think is the future of street art, how did it change in the past few years in your opinion?
I think, the future of street art is on the street, literally. We're surrounded by mile upon mile of dull, grey concrete in the form of roads and parking lots and no one or at least very few seem to want to touch it. Why? I know there's the whole convention of looking at art on a vertical plane but still: there's a certain reverance for the street, like it's untouchable or something, that I find mystifying. Maybe it has to do with the knowledge, that people take their cars really seriously and if you fuck with the sacred ground upon which they rely then they're going to go into a tizzy. Based on my recent experience this is indeed the case. Oh yeah, that reminds me of the other aspect of the future of street art: painting cars. I mean people have no problem putting tatoos on their bodies but when it comes to their cars (and there is as much steel in them as there is concrete on the road) it's like forget it. People freak, when you touch their cars. Nevermind that they're contributing to global warming, global conflict, pollution, health hazards in general and a generally dubious future for the world. Sacred the car is. It's the uniform, the business suit, the titanius layer of steel. Street art in my opinion seems to be more and more concerned with integrating itself with the immediate environment and I think, that this has become more evident in the last few years. I'm far from being an authority on the matter but this is the impression I get.

Five things you couldn't live without and why:
1. My family and friends, cause sometimes they know me better than I know myself.
2. Lovely ladies although I'd be happy with just one right now.
3. Laughs, cause you if you didn't laugh you'd cry.
4. Crying, cause you can't always laugh.
5. Coffee in the morning cause I'm grumpy and get a headache if I don't have one.

Things you don't like:
Car commercials, being put on hold and then getting the shitty music they play stuck in your head all day, heart break.

Any advise/last words:
take risks, ride your bike.

02

03

04

01 Bandoleer. Montreal, CAN. 2004
02 Valve. Boston, USA. 2004
03 Demon. Montreal, CAN. 2004
04 Light switch. Montreal, CAN. 2004

EROSIE

Eindhoven, NL

01

How rebellious is the art of putting up a sticker, stencil or a poster? I don't know. But what makes it more interesting to me is the reason for putting up something, the intention. For me working on the street has always been a way to work on developing my personal possibilities, my artistic scope, and my personal expression. It was in itself a reaction to the more conservative, strict graffiti-religion, but also graffiti for me used to be a way of expression, of finding and developing a personal language to communicate with. For me the development and growth of this personal expression is the goal, not so much the fact it's called graffiti or street art. Or should it be hardcore, all about keeping it real, underground, according to the latest sneaker-fashion or rebellious.
– Erosie. January, 2006

WWW.EROSIE.NET

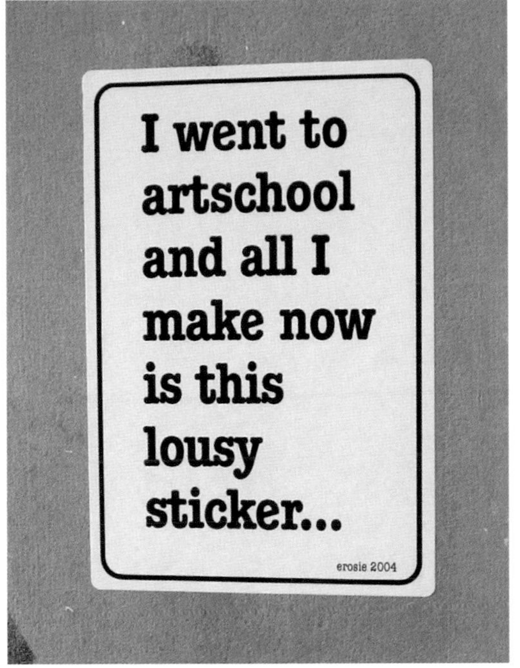

02

03

04

05

01 Eindhoven, NL. 2005
02 Eindhoven, NL. 2005
03 Eindhoven, NL. 2005
04 Eindhoven, NL. 2005
05 Eindhoven, NL. 2005

ELTONO

Madrid, ES

01

Eltono started with traditional graffiti in 1989, he got into urban experiments in 1997 and began his famous tuning forks in 1999. First the material he used was mostly acrylic paint, a brush and masking tape. In 2005 Eltono took his art one step further by starting sculptures work, called "Politonos". The first actions have been carried out in downtown Madrid. After years of painting and noticing, that there was a special response to his work, he decided to push the interaction level. So he acted exactly the same way as when painting but with a sculpture. He chose an adequate place and decided to install the sculpture on it. Then he hid and observed the scene and peoples reactions. He also worked with a video camera and a photographer so everything is getting documented from the beginning to the end.

The meaning of the artwork is "open your eyes and observe", "love yourneighborhood". He tries to bring art to places where people are not used to seeing it. He offers his art to the people who want to see it, he doesn't want to impose anything. That's the reason why his pieces are quite discreet. On the other side, when working in galleries, Eltono tries to get an inversed result as he tries to bring together gallery spectators and the streets.

Regarding the future of street art, Eltono sees future for people, who work in the street in an artistic and conceptual way. "It's not about graphic design street promotion, it's about art out of the canvas boundaries, using the city as an urban background."

WWW.ELTONO.COM

02

03

04

05

01-03, 04
Location: Madrid, ES. 2005

05
Location: Madrid, ES. 2005
Comment: The Politono got stolen and I recorded the whole action, it was so exiting!!!

Comments by Eltono. October, 2005
Photographs by Jorge Dominguez

NURIA
Madrid, ES

01

It comes about as a response to the mass communication into which we were born and that has always surrounded us. We have grown up right in the middle of a "social marketing" experiment and we are indoctrinated to such a degree, that they have managed to make us recognise a product without even mentioning it and what is even worse, they can communicate their brand to us simply by showing us a colour. I started painting on the street with Eltono in 1999, we had the same vision about the street and we wanted to react, to kick against this excessing information, this visual saturation by proposing a break from it all, but at the same time using their language. By painting simple and pure shapes I want to make people stop for a minute, observe and disconnect for a moment with that feeling.

It is our intention to give abandoned places a new function, namely that of providing an artistic backdrop and thereby creating a gallery on an urban scale.
– Nuria. December, 2005

02

03

04

05

01 Ileuhs, BRA. 2004
02 Tarifa, ES. 2002
03 Madrid, ES. 2005
04 Gumaraes, ES. 2005
05 Madrid, ES. 2002

FAILE

New York, USA

01

FAILE is a group of three artists from Canada, USA and Japan. We exchange sketch books and mix ideas together to create something which otherwise might not have been born. We work like a band... or like a DJ does: mix one song with other songs, like hip hop music made from sampled tracks, this is what we think is interesting about our style. We just love street art, traveling with friends and bombing...
– FAILE. November, 2005

WWW.FAILE.NET

02

03

04

01
Location: Las Vegas, USA. 2003
Comment: This trip was our first large-scale wheat-pasting trip in midwest USA. We enlarged the images and hand-painted at parent's garage in Phoenix AZ. Driving from AZ to LA and spent for 3days and nights, we found perfect spots such as an old gas station in the middle of Nevada desert and nicely big, old casino sign in Las Vegas. That day we remember it was mad windy and so difficult to put the papers up. In the strong gale it took all of us to hold it up so that the giant bunny boy wouldn't get blown away.
Medium: House paint, Paper, Wheat paste glue

02
Location: Barcelona, ES. 2004
Medium: House paint, spray paint and stencil

03
Location: Berlin, GER. 2004
Medium: House paint, spray paint and stencil

04
Location: Zurich, CH. 2004
Medium: House paint, spray paint and stencil

01

02

01
Location: Berlin, GER. 2004
Comment: Until late in the year 2003 we used to bring a whole bunch of hand-printed posters everywhere we traveled, which was kind of too much sometime. And also posters peel off easily when the winds and the rains hit. So after a while, we started cutting out stencils from the original posters. We figured out that it was much more convenient and that it gave us more difficult surface, such as metal, wood, stones and brick walls, to choose from. Of cource, the best thing is that it is more permanent. This is the FAILE stencil art gallery, entrance gate to a parking slot right next to where we were staying in Berlin.
Medium: House paint, spray paint and stencil

02
Location: London, UK. 2003
Medium: House paint, paper, silkscreen, wheat paste glue

03
Location: London, UK. 2003
Medium: House paint, paper, silkscreen, wheat paste glue

04
Location: Tokyo, JAP. 2004
Medium: House paint, spray paint and stencil

05
Location: Berlin, GER. 2004
Medium: House paint, spray paint and stencil

Comments by Faile. January, 2005

03

04

05

An Interview with Faile
Name: FAILE **Age:** 29-31 **Hometown:** Brooklyn NY
Cities where to find your art?
New York, London, Tokyo, Paris, Berlin, Amsterdam, Copenhagen and so on.
How did you come up with yor style, do you have a special message?
FAILE is a group of 3 artists from Canada, USA and Japan. We exchange sketch books and mix ideas together to create something which otherwise might not have been born. We work like a band... or like a DJ does: mix one song with other songs, like hip hop music made from sampled tracks, this is what we think is interesting about our style.
How did you get into street art?
In the late 90's, when one of us moved to NYC; he was fascinated by graffiti and street art. Soon after all of us got together and into street art, we killed downtown Manhattan with a shit load of wheat-pasting. The first street art project was hundreds of wheat-pasted hand-printed female nude posters.
Your favorite street artists:
Banksy, no doubt. He is a smart ass British ninja.
BAST. He is a super low-key guy but does super dope stuff. Good friend.
How does a typical day in your life look like?
Wake up, go to studio, phone calls and emails, lunch, work, dinner with friend or two, turn up music loud and paint, back home and chill with significance other.
Inspirations:
Traveling, seeing something new and meeting people. Old magazines, porn, movies and comics. Found materials such as old window frames, doors, papers and signs. Music.
Your favorite music:
Any kind of music as long as it makes us feel hot and sweaty.
Do you have any stories related to street art?
Yes, there are tons. From lovely ones to awful ones. Can't tell now.
What do you think is the future of street art, how did it change in the past few years in your opinion?
It's cool that people recognize street art as a popular art culture these days. Though, we never expected this explosion when we started because graffiti and street art had been around for ages already. Basically, we just love street art, travelling with friends, walking around, finding spots and bombing. It is more of a personal pleasure. And we still believe in the beauty of anonymous, shadowy figure. As long as people are digging it, it's fine. Even if people hate it, it's fine, too. It's natural.
Five things you couldn't live without and why:
1. LOVE
2. FRIENDS AND FAMILY
3. ART
4. TRAVEL
5. SEA FOOD
Things you don't like:
Cat Fight.

WWW.FAILE.NET

THUNDERCUT

New York. USA

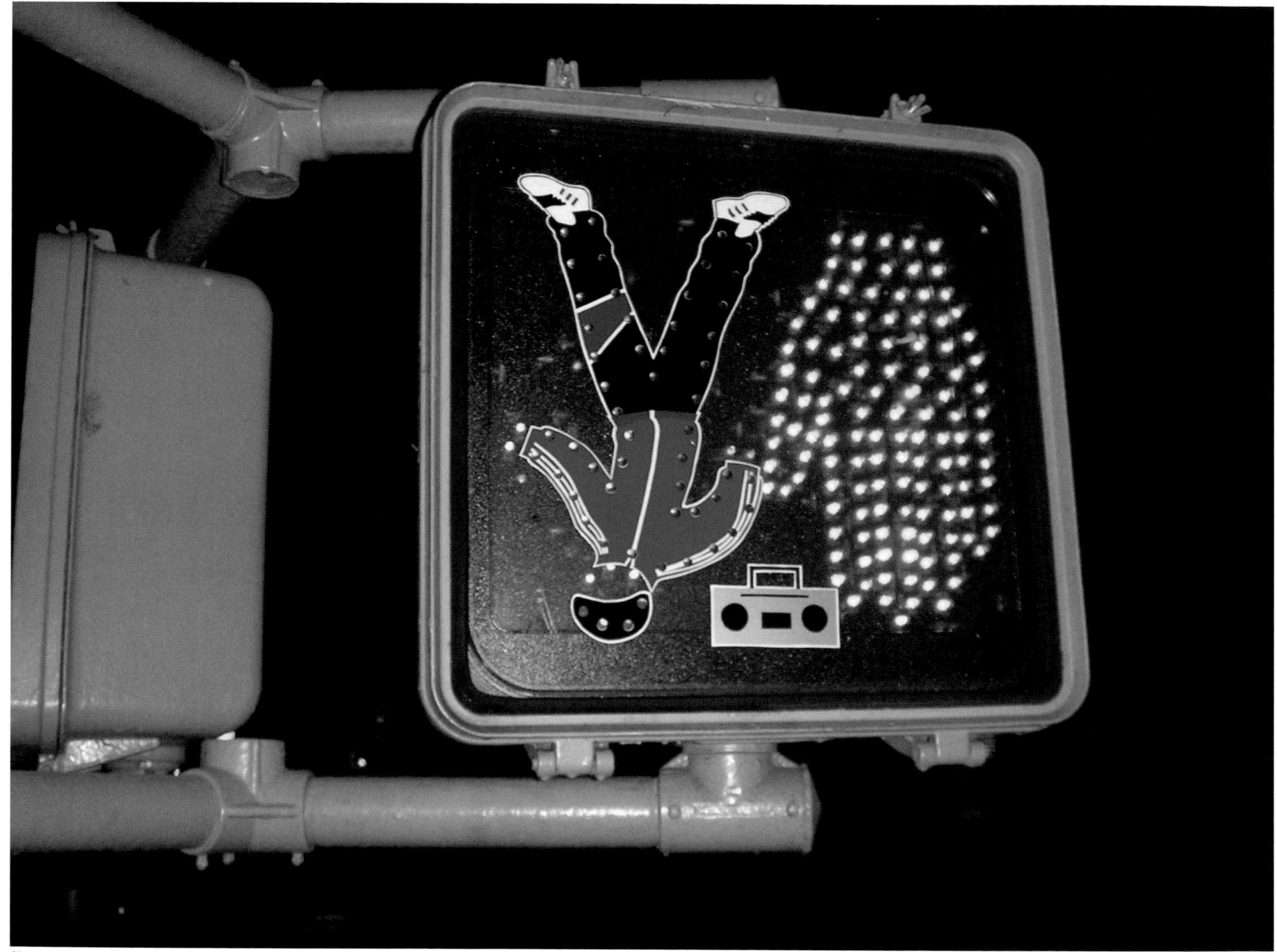

01

Thundercut is the creative outlet of two people who can't stop making things. From street based installations to pieces for gallery shows these two are never bored and rarely sleep. Their street work is intended to make people smile and is often times location specific. Utilizing a variety of materials and techniques these two are always coming up with clever ways to enhance the architecture of the city. They both like avocados, and despise canned peas.

WWW.THUNDERCUT.COM

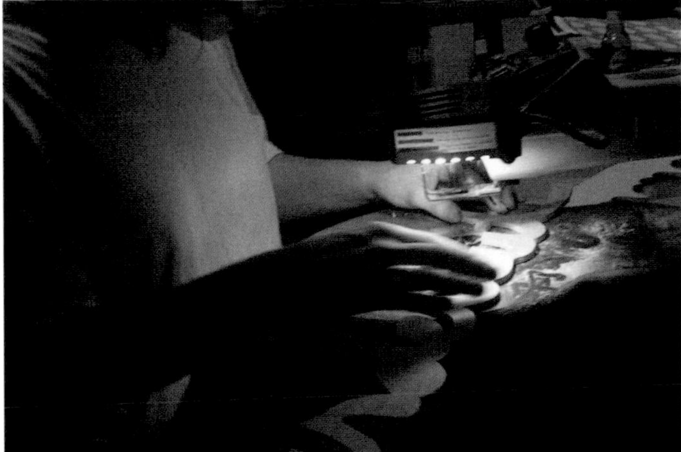

02

03

04

05

01
Location: East Village, New York, USA. 2005
Comment: Upon discovering a crosswalk sign installed upside down, Thundercut knew exactly what needed to be done. The sign was quickly turned into a skilled head-spinning breakdancer.

02
Location: Thundercut Studio, Brooklyn, New York, USA. 2005
Comment: With no graff skills but some obvious wood cutting skills, Thundercut pays homage to street art's graffiti roots. In their studio they prepare wood tags for late night missions.

03
Location: Brooklyn, New York, USA. 2005
Comment: This Trane is part of gang of conversion ehicles that cruise around the city. Keep an eye out, sometimes they travel in packs.

04
Location: Yankee Stadium, Bronx, New York, USA. 2005
Comment: The 2nd day of the Infamous Subway Series (when the Queensbased NY Mets play the Bronx based NY Yankees) brought fans from both teams pouring into Yankee stadium from all sides. Those arriving at Gate 6 were treated to a pre-game rivalry, the crosswalk signs on either side of the entrance were dressed for the occasion representing the competing teams. Although the Yankees failed to bring home a victory that day, the Subway Series "Crosswalk Competition" was decided by the fans leaving the game. The Mets Walker was left with only a shoe and half a hat while the Yankee Walker remained untouched and victorious.

05
Location: Pittsburgh, Pennsylvania, USA. 2005
Comment: The sea horse that coupled with a unicorn is an ultimate girlish delight and can be found blowing heart bubbles while swimming through many cities. This wooden creature often camouflages itself among the weeds of graffiti and urban decay.

Comments by Thundercut. January, 2006

MONSIEUR POULET

Toulouse, FR

01

02

03

04

05

06

07

08

01 Poster. Toulouse, FR. 2005
02 Poster. Toulouse, FR. 2005
03 Poster. Barcelona, ES. 2005
04 Poster. Toulouse, FR. 2005
05 Poster. New York, USA. 2005
06 Poster. New York, USA. 2005
07 Poster. New York, USA. 2005
08 Poster. Toulouse, FR. 2005

GALO

Amsterdam, NL

Originally from Milan in Italy, Galo now lives in Amsterdam. He very often works on projects with his friend Chaz from The London Police and was part of many urban art shows worldwide the last few years.

01 Sticker. Amsterdam, NL. 2004
02 World maps. Amsterdam, NL. 2004
03 Painting. Amsterdam, NL. 2004
04 Poster and Markers. Amsterdam, NL. 2004
05 Painting. Amsterdam, NL. 2004
06 Painting (with The London Police). Amsterdam, NL. 2004

WWW.SUBMULTIMEDIA.TV/GALOART

MISS VAN

Barcelona, ES

01

Miss Van started back in 1993, by painting controversial, sensual dolls onto street walls in Toulouse, France. Today her wall paintings and canvases – exhibited in art galleries in Paris, Barcelona, New York and Los Angeles – seem to arise from a surrealistic and colourful imagination, they are confusingly sweet and naive whilst at the same time seductive and voluptuously sexual, inviting the viewer to gaze whilst simultaneously warning them off with their confident, powerful expressions.

WWW.MISSVAN.COM

02

01 Canvas. Barcelona, ES. 2005
02 Latex paint. Barcelona, ES. 2005

PMH

London, UK

01

PMH loved art as a kid, but after having a bad teacher began to hate it and decided to give art up. In 2000 he started seeing stickers around London and soon hand painted his own. He then helped form the infamous Finders Keepers crew with D*face, Mysterious Al & Dave the Chimp. He has travelled over Europe with the crew, as well as holding it down with his personal stuff: painting and pasting, creating zines (inc. the Dilly), taking photos, writing, drawing and designing to name but a few. However it was only in 2005 that he started liking his own work, and he says everything up until then "is just practice".

WWW.FOTOLOG.NET/LAPMH WWW.FOTOLOG.NET/LAPMH2

02

03

04

05

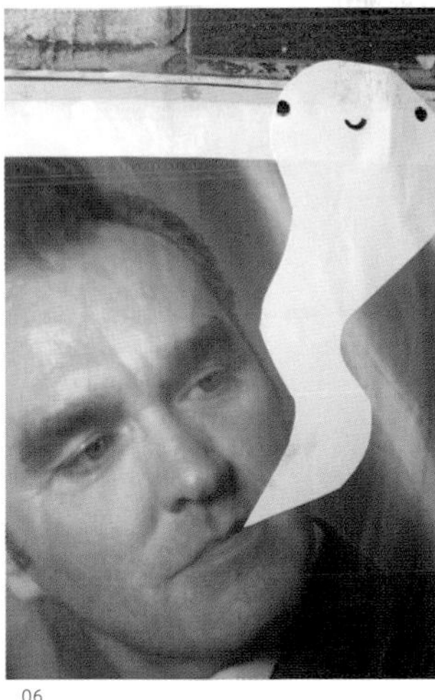
06

01 Graveyard. London, UK. 2005
02 Bubble gum. London, UK. 2005
03 Poster. London, UK. 2005
04 Stump. London, UK. 2005
05 Door. London, UK. 2005
06 Ghost. London, UK. 2005

DERRICK HODGSON

Toronto, CAN

01

Derrick Hodgson, grew up in the tiny village of Kettleby in southern Ontario and is currently living in Toronto, Ontario, Canada. His work can be found in cities such as Toronto, Montreal, Vancouver, L.A., Denver, New York, San Francisco, Tokyo, Berlin, Barcelona, Madrid. Derrick's style evolves from years of doodling and playing with line and is always evolving, often inspired from daily celestial freak outs. For him it's not so much being into street art as it is that he's into playing with the urban environment that he lives in... leaving little scribbles here and there that mostly go completely unnoticed...

His work doesn't have any special message, though politics can fuel some of his doodle sessions he sais, continuing with two quotes from Hundertwasser, "you are a guest of nature, behave" and "be independent, be careful, do not waste".

02

03

04

05

01 Latex paint. Toronto, CAN. 2005
02 Toronto, CAN. 2005
03 Exhibition. Toronto, CAN. 2005
04 Exhibition. Toronto, CAN. 2005
05 Illustration. 2005

WWW.MADREAL.COM

KORALIE
Montpellier, FR

01

HTTP://KOGAYLOU.FREE.FR

02

03

04

01 Poster. Montpellier, FR. 2005
02 At work. Latex paint. Montpellier, FR. 2005
03 Latex paint. Montpellier, FR. 2005
04 Poster. Montpellier, FR. 2005

C100

Munich, GER

01

C100 started with graffiti in '89 and got into urban art in 2001. When not busy in working on time-eating projects he enjoys putting up artwork on suitable places. He left his marks in cities such as London, Barcelona, Milan, Stockholm, Amsterdam and Rio de Janeiro.

WWW.C100STUDIO.COM

02

03

04

05

01
Location: Munich, GER. 2005
Comment: There is a Bavarian myth that there are some weird fantasy animals living in the woods, called "Wolperdinger". They are a mixture of various animals. I thought it would be a nice idea to put up some warning signs to heat up confusion.

02
Location: Rio de Janeiro, BRA. 2005
Comment: After I put up this poster with the help from my girlfriend, we took this nice nightshot. A few seconds after the photo was taken we were attacked by some Rio de Janeiro streetkids threwing stones at us. Nothing serious happened but still another experience.

03
Location: Munich, GER. 2005
Comment: Cardboard installation.

04
Location: Munich, GER. 2005
Comment: I put up the same poster in Barcelona where it was buffed the same night as a consequence of the city's "zero tolerance" attitude towards street art. How times change.

05
Location: Munich, GER. 2005

SOL CREW

Eindhoven. NL

01

SOL crew was founded in 1990 in Eindhoven, Netherlands. Since then the crew consisted of various people with a graffiti background finding very different ways of expression, either graffiti-wise using spraypaint and rollers, or using wood, latex, stickers or wheatpaste, you name it. Eindhoven has been a perfect visual playground to develop independently over the years because of a rich oldschool graffiti background on one side, and the distance from the bigger cities in The Netherlands on the other. Also the fact that there were different groups of people in one city developing simultaneously, like Betamaxxx, SOL crew, 031 and Space3 for instance. Nowadays the crew isn't a typical crew anymore, it split up into individuals doing their thing, but Late, Sektie, Zime, Erosie, Bomb, Lempke and Butch still keep inspiring each other to push their personal limits.

WWW.SOLCREW.NL

02

03

04

05

06

07

01 Ill Communication show. Manchester, UK. 2005
02 Artist: Zime. Barcelona, ES. 2005
03 Artist: Sektie. Eindhoven, NL. 2005
04 Artist: Bomb. Eindhoven, NL. 2005
05 Artist: Zime. London, E. 2005
06 Bomb Ross. Artist: Bomb. Eindhoven, NL. 2005
07 Artists: Late, Erosie, Butch, Bomb. Eindhoven, NL. 2005

EINE

London, UK

01

02

03

Coming from a traditional graffiti background London-based artist Eine painted a complete alphabet on various shutters in London. In total he painted 35 letters over a period of two months all in an area about five square miles. This project doesn't have a special idea but Eine takes photos of the letters and enjoys writing rude words with them. Since "the public have been predictably boring and the police have been thankfully stupid" he doesn't have any stories that happened while painting them. After this project he has started another font in a different part of London.

04

05

06

07

THE ART OF REBELLION 2

01-03 "Lazy, Fucking, Artists". Shutters. London, UK. 2005
04 "Hey, come on over". Latex paint, Spraypaint. London, UK. 2005
05 "Fucker".Sticker. London, UK. 2005
06 Poster, Spraypaint. London, UK. 2005
07 Spraypaint. India. 2005

56K

Hamburg, GER

01

56K, formerly known as GRAFFITILOVESYOU, lives and works in Hamburg, Germany. Starting with Graffiti in '93, he concentrated more on characters and urban experiments in '98. The alias origins from slow Internet connections via 56K modems and symbolizes simpleness and compression in figuration and the human need to keep things slow once in a while. In his works on the streets he displays strange characters and odd situations as a result of daily observations and ideas generated out of modern city life. With the traffic sign works and the imitation of famous corporate logos he focusses on the human tendency to be directed by orders and symbols that appear official and authoritarian and not to question them.

02

03

04

01
Location: Hamburg, GER. 2004
Comment: "AMATEURS". After two guys in the bus discussing about something neither of them understood. Both had very precise opinions.

02
Location: Berlin, GER. 2004
Comment: Two fake roadsigns for "road to nowhere-the great urban art swindle" exhibition at the Lovelite, Berlin.

03
Location: Hamburg, GER. 2005
Comment: "YOU ARE NOT HERE".

04
Location: Hamburg, GER. 2004
Comment: "PUBLIC SERVICE". Everyday I hate every graffiti everywhere very much. Fled the scene.

Comments by 56K. January, 2006

WWW.000-56K.DE

KLISTERPETE

Stockholm, SE

01

02

03

Klisterpete's birdhouse installations can be found all over Stockholm, where he has set up 117 wooden houses on traffic signs and lamp-posts. They are built of wood, each one uniquely crafted and painted to resemble a variety of objects, from birds to portraits.

There's a pole at the base of the houses which fits into the top of the traffic signs, sometimes glue is used for added stability. The houses are usually installed during daytime. Passers-by witness in wonder a 30-year-old man climbing up a traffic light.
Nevertheless numerous birds probably thank him for his mission.
– Kid Pele. January, 2006

04

05

06

07

01 Bird. Stockholm, SE. 2004
02 Girl. Stockholm, SE. 2004
03 Factory. Stockholm, SE. 2004
04 Copy (check the house in the background). Stockholm, SE. 2004
05 Traffic sign. Stockholm, SE. 2004
06 Village. Stockholm, SE. 2004
07 Traffic light. Stockholm, SE. 2004

AKAY

Stockholm, S

01

02

03

04

Ridiculous sums of money are spent producing bronze sculptures. Honoring heroes and artists on Stockholm's street corners. Akay's concrete sculptures give tribute to the invisible citizens, they offer a reminder of more affordable solutions to a problem. People approach the sculptures with caution, so life like. Is it real? It's not real. Some gather around to kick a man when he's down.
This is real.
– Kid Pele. January, 2006

WWW.AKAYISM.ORG

BARSKY*

Stockholm, S

05

06

07

The city is a playground. Set down your shopping bags. Swing.

Swing from bridges. Swing from bus stops.
Swing after you crossed the street at a crosswalk.
Backwards. Forwards. Look around.
Barsky has been to your part of town.

Take a bit of rope. Abandoned tires.
Anything you can find.
Hang your junk up from bridges.
Tie them tight to traffic signs.

Swing into oncoming traffic.
Wave to people passing by.
The city is your playground. Do you need to ask them why?

01 Akay. Stockholm, SE. 2005
02 Akay. Stockholm, SE. 2005
03 Akay. Stockholm, SE. 2005
04 Akay. Stockholm, SE. 2005
05 Barsky. Stockholm, SE. 2004
06 Barsky. Stockholm, SE. 2004
07 Barsky. Stockholm, SE. 2004

*Barsky is the collaboration between Klisterpete and Akay, two friends getting things done in Stockholm's streets. Words by Kidpele. January 2006.

YOU ARE BEAUTIFUL

Chicago, USA

01

You Are Beautiful is a simple, powerful statement, which is incorporated into the over absorption of mass media and lifestyles, that are wrapped in consumer culture.

This statement and the context in which someone finds it gives meaning to its message and purpose to this project. The intention behind this project is to reach beyond ourselves as individuals to make a difference by creating moments of positive self realization in those, who happen across the statement: You Are Beautiful. Intention is the most important aspect of the You Are Beautiful project in its idea of purity. Graffiti and street art are an act not a style, but stylistically large corporations have been copying and using the "urban decay" look to sell products. It all comes down to intention. Nothing is sacred. Everything, that has a perceived value becomes commodified. Companies hire out teenagers to slap up stickers and posters and pay their fines when they are caught by the police. This is not street art, but a marketing campaign. The reasons why street artists are doing what they are doing, in the way that they are doing, is not simply to question their surroundings; but to provide alternative perspectives, meanings, or values to those of consumerism. Advertising elicits a response to buy, where this project elicits a response to do something. The attempt with You Are Beautiful is to create activism instead of consumerism. You Are Beautiful uses the medium of advertising and commercialization to spread a positive message. Projects like these make a difference in the world by catching us in the midst of daily life and creating moments of positive self realization.

WWW.YOU-ARE-BEAUTIFUL.COM

02

03

04

05

01 Styrofoam Cups. Chicago, USA. 2004
02 Wood. Chicago, USA. 2004
03 Printed Paper. Chicago, USA. 2004
04 Tar Paper. Chicago, USA. 2004
05 Steel & Paper. Chicago, USA. 2004

DAVE THE CHIMP

London, UK

01

WWW.DAVETHECHIMP.CO.UK

02

03

04

01
Location: Hackney, East London, UK. 2004
Comment: When I started painting in the streets in 1998 my work was mostly "site specific", each piece created for the specific site it was being painted at, and this remains the same today. The piece above, "Hackney Harbour", perfectly illustrates what I mean by "site specific". As soon as I saw this spot on Hackney Road, East London, I noticed the brick stairs and imagined a harbour, and knew immediately that I had to paint a pirate and an octopus.
With much of my street work there is a meaning or a message hidden behind the cuteness and humour. This piece was painted while the girl I loved was away in Mexico for three months, and the message was to keep an eye on what's important to you, and not get distracted by false beauty and desire. Ironically, at the time I was painting this, my girlfriend was spreading her legs for a crack addict surfer. Such is the life of a pirate!

02
Location: Bethnal Green Road, East London, UK. 2005
Comment: I was finishing the outline on this piece at 4:30 on a Monday morning when a Police car pulled up behind me (there was a big NY style crack down on graffiti at that time in London).
"Do you have permission to do that?" the male cop asked me.
"Yes" I replied, suddenly becoming the worlds greatest liar.
"I work for an advertising company, and this is one of the new characters we've created for McDonalds to replace Ronald McDonald and Hamburgular. We've paid the shop owner so we can paint on his wall. It's all part of a new "street promotion."
"Is it a banana?" PC Einstein asks.
"I'm not sure what it is, I don't work on the character development side, I just paint it on the wall."
"What's its name then?"
"Like I said, I don't work on character development, I'm not sure if any of them have names yet."
"So, if you have permission, why are you painting at night?"
"That's the whole point. If I painted this during the day people would see me, and the idea is that these new characters just appear over night."
By this time the female cops in the back seat are giggling away, but they bought the story, and decided to leave me to it. I finished my outlines, a little shakey, then laughed all the way home. Suckers!

03
Location: City Road, London, UK. 2004
Comment: "Where Is God?" Hand painted poster.

04
Location: Bethnal Green, London, UK. 2005
Comment: "Pierced Ear Punk"

05
Location: Whitechapel, London. UK. 2005
Comment: "It's Not Where You've Been, It's Where You're Going"

Comments by Dave the Chimp, January, 2006

05

STEFAN MARX

Hamburg, GER

01

Stefan Marx lives in a small flat over a bridge in Hamburg. His roommates are talking french fries, mountains wearing hats, skatable houses and farting airplanes. Together, there is nothing to do but drawing. The Lousy Livincompany is his old-age pension, doing zines with drawings, photos and notes from time to time is a good thing to do for him, too.

02

03

04

05

07

06

08

09

01
Location: Smallville record store. Hamburg, GER. 2005
Comment: Drawing for the release of the upcomming new ISOLÉE Record "We are monster" on the store windows, I did the artwork for this record.
Photos by Jan Baedeker
Medium: Acryl on window

02
Location: Fishmarket. Hamburg, GER. 2005
Comment: Willow did a wallride on this skateable house sculpture I built. He is an amazing skateboarder.
Photo by David Böttger
Medium: Wodden sculpture

03
Location: Barcelona, ES. 2005
Comment: I did this huge painting for the "Skateboardfieber" exhibition in Barcelona.

04-08,
Location: Hamburg, GER
Comment: Photos by Nice Guy.

09
Location: London, UK. 2005
Comment: I think Dave the Chimp wrote this slogan on this wall a year ago .

BAR BRASSERIE
MOUFLE

G*

Paris, FR

G*, originally from Cannes, is famous for his big scale paste-ups on countless billboards and walls all over Paris. The posters' motives are mainly oversized enlargements of photos he took while exploring the city seeking for special moments to ban on film.

They range from people in daily life situations to old cars to observation cameras, to name just a few. All photos are taken with a 35mm camera, he never uses digital cameras as he likes the incalculability and the limitations of traditional photography which gives them their very original look. Most of his work can be found in Paris only because "he doesn't practise Artourism".

01 Poster. Paris, FR. 2005

01

02

03

04

05

01 "Non.Conforme". Paris, FR. 2005
02 Marseilles, FR. 2004
03 "Mobile". Paris, FR. 2005
04 "I see you". Paris, FR. 2004
05 "Vous me plaise". Paris, FR. 2004. Photo by Jérôme Vallin.

MOONDOG LOVES YOU

London.UK

01

02

Lloyd Ellis is a London-based cartoonist and illustrator, who leaves small bits of cardboard with drawings on them, all around the world in an attempt to make people smile. In clubs, cracks in walls or on lampposts etc. people find them, visit the website and are sent more so they can help spread the love. Recycling as many cardboard boxes as he can, he draws with Tipp-Ex and marker, making them on the move, whenever and wherever he wants; the world is his studio. They have now found their own higher purpose and has become a kind of accidental cult, producing street art that can be friendly, bio-degradable and taken home by people if they want. Lloyd would love you to be his friend.
– Lloyd Ellis. January, 2006

01 London, UK. 2005
02 London, UK. 2005

WWW.MOONDOGLOVESYOU.COM

JUSTIN KEES

Amsterdam, NL

01

02

Justin Kees has been into street art for many years doing various actions like putting up posters or installing little character-like looking tiny cans on trees or walls. Originally from Los Angeles he now resides in Amsterdam working an various projects like the "Pigs before Swine" project he organised in 2005.

01 Amsterdam, NL. 2005
02 Amsterdam, NL. 2005

ADAM NEATE
London, UK

01

I started leaving paintings in the street in 1997-98. So far I have left over four thousand individualy painted works. My mission...err...to never create the same image twice.
– Adam Neate. January, 2006

02

03

04

05

01 London, UK. 2005
02 London, UK. 2005
03 London, UK. 2005
04 London, UK. 2005
05 London, UK. 2005

CHANOIR

Barcelona, ES

01

HTTP://CHANOIR.FREE.FR

02

03

04

05

06

01 Spraypaint. Paris, FR. 2005
02 Spraypaint. Barcelona, ES. 2005
03 Spraypaint. Barcelona, ES. 2005
04 Spraypaint. Barcelona, ES. 2005
05 Spraypaint. Barcelona, ES. 2005
06 Spraypaint. Barcelona, ES. 2005

NOMAD

Berlin, GER

01

02

03

04

05

01 Berlin, GER. 2004
02 Berlin, GER. 2004
03 Berlin, GER. 2004
04 Yoyogihase. Berlin, GER. 2005
05 Reykjavik, ISL. 2005

D*FACE
London, UK

01

Like a snail leaving its sticky trail, London based street artist D*Face leaves his artwork; stickers, posters, marker drawings on empty advertising space & discarded objetcs, always on the lookout for that ultimate spot. D*face sees every smooth surface as his exhibition space, hanging his work at every opportunity. The higher, the cleaner the spot, the better the gallery, which guarantees a longer show! He wants people to be intrigued by these faces peering down at them on every street corner, to question their relationship with the work, why it's there and to encourage the viewer to not just "look" but to see their surroundings, and to put a smile or frown on their face!

WWW.DFACE.CO.UK

02

03

04

05

01
Location: London. UK. 2005
Comment: Big D*. Emulsion. Roller. Spray paint.
Numerous taggers. There's alot to be said for scale.
This piece stands at over 15ft in height and took several litres of white paint and a dodgy ladder to complete.
Due to it's location and the vast amount of white space, I knew it wouldn't run clean for long, it didn't. I returned about 6 months later to find it battered with tags, the layering of tags had a beautiful quality so I used this as the fill, it made the piece even better and gave it a quality that would be hard to replicate.

02
Location: Milan, I. 2005
Comment: My army. Pasted poster. The overhang from the balcony was a near exact fit for the poster, protecting it from the elements, but I don't think from the scrapers or other fly posters!

03
Location: London, UK. 2005
Comment: Ugly brother. London. Spray paint. This piece was painted in an old water cleaning plant and a favourite spot for artists. The floor is littered with cans from years of painting, making for an amazing carpet and foreground.

04
Location: Soho, London, UK. 2005
Comment: Lab Mice. Hand cut MDF wood, painted with enamels. Bonded in place. I released loads of these mice back into their natural environment after a daring raid on the lab, where they were held captive, they had been subjected to years of experimentation. Normally used to test the effects of inks and spray paint. Mouse on the left is instructing second mouse to draw. He would have drawn a cat, which I went back to execute two days later. But mouse two had been taken, or fled the scene.

05
Location: Barcelona, ES. 2004
Comment: Hang of God. Pasted poster. Hitting the center of this arch/ bricked up shop gave a good composition and context for the poster. I like the woman on the end walking by, she thinks I'm taking a photo of her and goes to adjust her hair.

Comments by D*Face. October, 2005

DAN WITZ

New York, USA

01

02

03

Dan Witz first started doing street art when he moved to New York City in the late 1970's. Every summer since then he has done some kind of anonymous non-permissional outdoor piece. His projects have had varying agendas-aesthetic, socio-political, and personal but the main motivation has always been getting out of the studio and having fun–to make work that's pure, direct, and uncompromised.

His two main early influences were punk culture and the urban blight of his surroundings. Art had to be challenging and wildly impractical or he wasn't interested. Galleries were the status quo and therefore the problem. He is still attracted to music and art that goes against the stream. Actually he needs it more than ever to help him stay awake.

With the rise in real estate prices in NYC, and the consequent lowering of tolerance for street art, his installation strategies have had to evolve out of neccesity. Early on he used to spend hours on one piece, standing there painting with tiny brushes. Beginning in the 1990's, with the police cracking down and graffiti becoming a felony, he needed to either work in less trafficked areas or get out of there faster. That's when he started using stickers he'd make at home and integrating them into the wall with an airbrush. Now, the maximum time he spends on site could be less than 60 seconds. He works from a portable studio in the saddlebags of his motorcycle. Before anyone knows what's happened he's usually already gone, weaving thru traffic.

WWW.DANWITZSTREETART.COM

04

05

06

01 Skateboarder. New York, USA. 2005
02 Hands. New York, USA. 2005
03 Light. New York, USA. 2005
04 Rolls. New York, USA. 2005
05 Dan at work. New York, USA. 2005
06 Colobri. New York, USA. 2005

ASBESTOS

Dublin, IRL

01

Using a wide range of mediums including paste-ups, stickers, stencils, painted photography, monosodium glutamate and acrylic transfer, Asbestos has spread his toxic cloud across Europe and beyond over the last few years. His art transports passers by from the blinkered safety of their daily routines. Pictures of dolls heads captured by him in a dolls hospital in Amsterdam have become one of the central icons in his arsenal. These dolls heads have manifested themselves as posters, paintings and more recently painted pieces of plaster, battered and gold leafed. In the world of Asbestos his dolls represent innocence, their eyes blindfolded from the evil of the world – lonely icons of lost souls. Conversely, his series of Lost posters pleads with the public to help find lost jugs, photos of dogs, slippers, kettles of fish and other mundane items no one would miss in the first place. The question he poses is how obsessed are we with possessions? More recently he has been photographing homeless people and then painting their portraits on discarded pieces of wood which are put back up on the streets. These portraits capture their lonely silent dignity that's often ignored by society. If that ain't enough for the baying masses, he finds time to organise the world's biggest Secret Santa Swap for street artists across the globe.

02

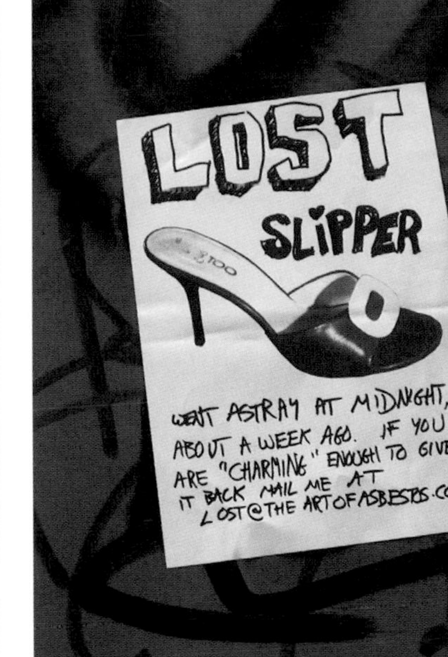

03

04

05

01
Location: New York, a Secret Santa gift for Faile (it never made it back to the street), USA. 2005
Comment: This piece is an acrylic transfer painting of a photography taken in the Pigalle area of Paris. A homeless woman lies sleeping with her old yet angelic face peeking out. I can only hope that she is dreaming of somewhere else.

02
Location: Public toilet, Broadwick St. London, UK. 2005
Comment: One of 40 gold leafed dolls put up around Soho. They get two reactions–people think they're cute or they're really freaked out by these.

03
Location: Dublin, IRL. 2004
Comment: One person claimed to have found this slipper, but all attempts to return the footwear have failed to this date.

04
Location: Dublin, IRL. 2003
Comment: A monosodium Glutamate stencil of a flamingo worked onto a drunken photo taken in a New York cab.

05
Location: Sydney, AU. 2005
Comment: One of four painted canvases for the Jeremyville Sketchel show. This five legged Icelandic pony is the first animal in the distorted animal series and was inspired by a meeting with French photographer Yann Arthus Bertrand in Reykjavík.

Comments by Asbestos. January 2006

M-CITY
Gdynia, PL

01

27-year-old Marius Waras started cutting stencils 13 years ago. His project M-city is about the right of people to create public space. The project criticizes the build up of cities which are created by architects, urbanists, corporations, and politicians. The inspiration to the architecture of M-city came mostly from the architecture of Threecity (Gdansk, Sopot, Gdynia, Baltic sea, north of Poland) and its surroundings, but there's no avoiding of motifs from other regions of Poland. The architecture of the town is in a sense a promotion of groups of people who work together for society. These include independent media, charities, non-governmental organisations, theatres etc. Most of the project's realisations are on specially chosen walls and match the historical or architectural context of the surroundings. The people on the stencils are mostly the author's friends or persons involved in some local social activity.

The first step of preparation is a sketch of a given building on A4 paper drawn in isometric perspective and inscribed into a couple of cubes one on top of the other. Due to this technique printing the stencil is much easier, moreover it allows printing a single fragment of the building. All of the buildings can be connected in multiple ways with the author's imagination as the only limit. It's easy to customise the buildings by mixing the roofs and elevations–parts of different stencils. All of the objects have a brighter left face and a darker right face, which adds depth and vividness. After the sketch is done it's enlarged to A2 format and laminated on both sides. This guarantees long-term resilience of the stencil, keeping it from absorption of the paint. As the layers of the paint get quite thick it's easy to tear them off and use the stencil again (some of the stencils were used hundreds of times). Finally the stencil is cut out.

02

03

04

05

06

07

01 Billboard. Gdynia, PL. 2005
02 Bridge Pier. Gdynia, PL. 2005
03 Billboard. Gdynia, PL. 2005
04 Bridge Pier. Gdynia, PL. 2005
05 Stone. Gdynia, PL. 2005
06 Wall. Gdynia, PL. 2005
07 Harbour. Gdynia, PL. 2005

DARIUS & DOWNEY

New York, USA

01

02

Leon Reid (a.k.a. Darius Jones) and Brad Downey began working collaboratively in Brooklyn, NY at the turn of the 21st Century. Their work is characterized by the use of common street objects as the basis for their art and the clever appropriation of reflective work vests to serve as disguise for daytime installations.

Reid's involvement in street art goes back to his adolescence while tagging VERBS in his native Cincinnati, OH. Downey studied classical drawing and painting in Atlanta, GA, before beginning his documentary film on street art "Public Discourse". The film captured Reid's transformation to Darius Jones and the beginning steps of the Darius and Downey collaboration.

03

04

05

06

07

01 Leon Reid (Darius Jones). "It's All Right". Brooklyn, NYC, USA. 2005
02 Leon Reid (Darius Jones). "The Kiss". London, UK. 2004.
03 Leon Reid (Darius Jones) at work in Brooklyn, NYC, USA. 2005
04 Leon Reid (Darius Jones) at work in Bristol, UK. 2004
05 Brad Downey. "A Father's Duty". London, UK. 2004
06 Leon Reid (Darius Jones) and Brad Downey. "Sit your Arse Down". London, UK. 2004
07 Leon Reid (Darius Jones). "Chainsnake". New York, USA. 2005

L'ATLAS

Paris, FR

01

WWW.LATLAS.NET

02

03

L'ATLAS started his career by carving his name into the tables with a pair of compasses in primary school and spent his youth spraying the streets of Paris, Marseille, Toulouse, Barcelona, Madrid, Lisbon...His name is known as far as Morocco where he learned the classical Arabian calligraphy taught by a local master. Since then he is mixing the Latin typography with this tradition of gesture. Back in Paris he worked in a cinema and learned how to cut movies; he produced documentary movies about the profession of gesture (metiers du geste), in which he integrated street art.

The next step brought him to Egypt to film a Syrian calligrapher, who taught him to violate the traditional (established) rules: Mixing typography, architecture and logotype. All this enriched forms and ideas of his arising art. Ensuing an odyssey through the labyrinth of old cities of the Middle East (Cairo, Damascus, Istanbul, Aleph).

Right now he is working on: big posters (4 x 3m), which he glues onto advertising panels, north bounded compasses fused onto the sidewalks and a series of painted canvases, he promised to exhibit them after he travelled around the world.

L'ATLAS developed this art without a name, which unites drawing and writing. His logos are based on words or phonemes deformed into ideograms. Through this a new form of a universal language is created which combines writing and drawing, sense and form, idea and intuition. L'ATLAS seeks for a balance between body and soul, consciousness and subconciousness, Orient and Occident.

01 Photo by Emilie Garnaud. Paris, FR. 2005
02 Jakharta, IND. 2005
03 Paris, FR. 2005

MATT SEWELL

Manchester, UK

01

29- year-old Matt Sewell is part of the internationally well-known Scrawl collective, a group of artists doing exhibitions worlwide. His cute girls and fluffy animals are inspired by nature and animals. Other sources of inspirations are Tove Janson, Winsor McKay, Pat Hutchins, Jiri Trnka, Klaus Haapaneimi, Paul Rand, Erja Hirvi, Eames and Max Sendak. His style comes from his sketchbook, which comes from the centre of the triangle between hand, head and heart, he sais. He is working as an illustrator adapting characters and daft sketches for the clients like Big Issue, The Guardian, Playstation 2.

WWW.MATTSEWELL.CO.UK

02

03

04

01 Spraypaint. Manchester, UK. 2005
02 Fox. Spraypaint. Manchester, UK. 2005
03 Poster. Manchester, UK. 2005
04 Spraypaint. Manchester, UK. 2005

KLUB7
Halle, GER

01

02

03

Klub7 is a creative collective, whose main rule is that there is no rule. There is just one big playground: the city. With the intention to create a relationship between them and the city they design the open space to make it a place everyone feels good in. On their steady search for new ways to express they try various techniques such as sticking, installing, designing–always keen for new possibillities. They communicate, provoke, think, attack, respect – they destroy borders and create new ones. All in all Klub7 creates collages onto the citie's surface to mark their territory. Their quality level is constantly high. Klub7 wants their ideas to be understood immediately, which is the reason for the transparency and an easy understanding of their work.
– Klub7. Halle/Saale, GER. Summer 2005

04

05

06

07

01 (with Tower from Berlin) Tillburg, NL. 2005
02 Halle, GER. 2005
03 Halle, GER. 2005
04 Berlin, GER. 2005
05 Berlin, GER. 2005
06 Berlin, GER. 2005
07 Berlin, GER. 2005

BÉLA JANSSEN

Hamburg, GER

01

02

03

In contrast to his street art work in his three gallery exhibitions to far, Béla Janssen has used installations to explore the technical and narrative possibilities of the cassette tape.

The definitive characteristic of the castette, i.e. to archive sound on audio tape, inspired Béla to translate this phenomenon into an interior environment. That was the genus of the first installation, which consisted of a continuous sound loop of a birdsong coming from a tape in a walkman suspened by transparent threads from above, so that both casette and strip of audio tape appeared to be floating in the air. The shadow of the "flying" cassette on the ceiling particularly unscored the poetic, animate quality of the cassette tape.

01
Location: Hinterkonti. Hamburg, GER. 2005
Comment: "Travel taping Guatemala, Costa Rica" exhibition. Photo by Jonas Gerhard

02
Location: Livingston, GUA. 2005
Comment: "Taping Central America" group exhibition.

03
Location: Hamburg, GER. 2005
Comment: "Flying cassette" group exhibition.

MORCKY.BWOY

Amsterdam.NL

01

02

01
Location: Amsterdam, NL. 2004
Comment: This was the very first speaker action I did. The spot is in the old city, near central station. I always take my time painting as I need to feel the spot and the time to visualize how the shapes are going to fit on the surface. And also to check if the place is quiet or not. While checking out a friend of mine was biking by and saw me standing weirdly on the sidewalk doing nothing at 6 a.m.
He stopped and asked whether I was alright and offered me a place to crush. I told him I was alright. Thanks Pete.

02
Location: Amsterdam, NL. 2004
Comment: This spot was so clear in my mind. I have drawings where I had completely planned everything. A perfect flat surface perpendicular to the streets. There were a lot of positive reactions for this one. Actually the piece was planned to be continued on the right side but a vespa was parked there that night..

Amsterdam-based artist Galman who origins from Italy has been writing graffiti since 2000 under the name Morcky. The big speaker boxes are a document of nights full of no sleep, loud beats and spraypaint.

BORIS HOPPEK
Barcelona, ES

01

Coming originally from Siegen in Germany Boris has been living in Barcelona for a few years. Besides doing art on the street he works on various other projects and exhibitions worldwide. He's busy creating characters and creatures, which he varies in a continual process as dolls, installations, animation and graffiti using different materials.
His lovely Bimbo dolls of cannibals, Hitler and Klukluxklan figures already gained cult status.

WWW.BORISHOPPEK.DE

02

03

04

05

01 Cardboard boxes, spraypaint. Zaragoza, ES. 2005
02 Cardboard boxes, spraypaint. Barcelona, ES. 2005
03 "Gratis". Spraypaint. Barcelona, ES. 2005
04 Chalk drawings. Barcelona, ES. 2005
05 Chalk drawings. Barcelona, ES. 2005

CUM*

Gent, BE

01

Based in Ghent, Belgium, the trio known as Cum* has been doing their "fucking erotic street entertainment" since 2002. Their work began with a stencil of a pin-up girl and has evolved, with a great deal of influence by the massive amounts of pornography readily available on the Internet, into a sexual free for all. Liberating the ladies from their computer monitor confines and setting them loose on the streets, Cum* was curious to see what would become of the girls when taken out of context. Originally a project slated just for the streets, Cum* has also moved indoors where they have more artistic freedom to experiment with their explicit subject matter. Using a color scheme of mostly black, white and pink, silk screened images of the girl-next-door types are juxtaposed with drip-heavy spray painted stencils of Russ Meyer looking women. On canvas, both the Madonna and the Whore are celebrated and they coexist side by side with neither camp passing judgment on the other.
– Liberation Iannillo. January, 2006

WWW.CUMINTHESTREETS.COM

02

03

04

01 Poster. Gent, BE. 2005
02 Poster. Gent, BE. 2005
03 Poster. Gent, BE. 2005
04 Stencil. Gent, BE. 2005

TABAS

Marseilles, FR

01

Tabas is 31-year-old French graphic-designer and artist, named Cédric Malo's. While living in sunny Marseilles, he started with traditional graffiti and became a house hold name in the international street art scene. In January 2000 he created his own Tabasstudio , a French print & interactive design agency. French design publication Pyramid released a book about his work in 2005 within their series design&designers, "No.24 Tabas". The name Tabas is a French slang expression for "ça tabasse !", which means "it bits up!" His logo is also a divertment of the logo of french tobacco sellers.

WWW.TABAS.FR

02

05

03

04

An Interview with Tabas
Name: Tabas **Age:** 31 **Hometown:** Marseilles in the sunny South of France
Cities where to find your art?
Marseilles, London, Clermont Ferrand, Paris, Nantes, Berlin, Annecy, Barcelona, Valence, Toulon, New York ...
How did you get into street art and why?
I don't really remember, sometimes, I drink too much.
How did you come up with yor style, do you have a special message?
Buy my book at http://www.artdesign.fr, designdesigners tabas N°24
look at http://www.bureaudetabas.com
Your favorite street artists and why:
I'm keen on the work of: Akroe, Alexone, Gomes, Flying Fortress, Krsn, Miss Van, because they've send me money to say so.
Other interests:
70's orange objects, eating apples, taking photos, walking on the grass, travelling around the world, eating pastas...
How does a typical day in your life look like?
I wake up, drink orange juice, jump on my bike to go to my desk room, open my apple computer, stretch my fingers, close the computer, eat good things, watch some TV, sleep with my naked girlfriend.
Inspirations:
They are based on my daily urban life. All the things I've done, all the people I've met, all the places I've seen...I'm used to taking pictures and reminisce.
Your favorite music:
The song of the wind in the trees.

Do you have any stories related to street art?
Once upon a time there was a fledging bird who didn't know yet how to fly.
One night in deep winter, he feel out his nest onto footpath. So he started to squawk "Peeoo! Pee-oo! Pee-oo!" until his gullet ached, because it was deathly cold. And then to this delight, along come a cow. She saw him and wanted to warm him up. So she lifted up her tail and – splat! A great big streaming pat landing on him. Now nice and cosy and warm, the birdie poked out his little head and started squawking "PEE-OO! PEE-OO! PEE-OO! PEE-OO!" even louder than before. But then an old coyote came racing up, stretched out a paw, extracted the birdie from this sticky predicament, wiped him clean, and...YUM! One mouthful and he was gone...
My grand father used to say there a moral to this story, but that everyone has to find it himself. For me it's the moral of a new area.
Those, who put you in the shit aren't always trying to hurt you, and those who get you out aren't always trying to help.
But more than anything: When you're in the shit, shut up!
What do you think is the future of the street art ?
I vision commercial exploitation of our work by famous brands.
How did it change in the past few years in your opinion?
I used to think it would make me rich and famous...and I was right ;-))
Five things you could'nt live without:
taking pictures, the sun, looking at attractive beautiful women, sleeping over in the morning, the grass, apples, eating yogurts, taking free time, 70's colours

Things you don't like:
Stupid yelling people, girls with hairy armpit, computer's breakdown bombs, disease, graffiti and street art, cold rain...
Any advise/ Last words:
Send me money ! I'm fed up with working ;-))

06

01 Spraypaint. Clermont Ferrand, FR. 2004
02 Poster Siao+Ciel. Valence, FR. 2004
03 Handmade dolls. "saccage" Bird. Marseilles, FR. 2004
04 Handmade dolls. "lepetit l'apeint " Rabbit. Marseilles, FR. 2004
05 Poster. Marseilles, FR. 2004
06 Tabas logo. Marseilles, FR. 2004

FUCK YOUR CREW
Berlin, GER

01

FUCK YOUR CREW choose their name as a provocative comment on a bullshit hiphop-attitude. What began with putting up underwear to destroy-lines lead into a project that should only expose the fun of drawing and experimenting with techniques and spaces. According to their approach they found it more important to produce original pieces that show their love to experiment than to spread their name by simple copy and paste. The best thing that could happen in their minds is to cause a constructive reaction on their provocation and if it's only a smile in the face of the passer-by.

02

03

04

05

06

07

08

09

01-09 Berlin, GER. 2005

BUDDY LEMBEK

Los Angeles, USA

01

Whether you're viewing one of Buddy Lembek's video pieces under his Blond Chili Productions label or stumbling across his street art, you will most likely find his work to be solid, colorful, sloppy, disgusting at times and most often humorous. Lembek is always creating colorful and funny characters in a variety of mediums. Many times installing his work while in costume, and appearing in his films and live performances as original characters. His work is often inspired by poor advertising, pop culture, public access TV, Middle-America, and current events.

WWW.BLONDCHILI.COM

02

03

04

05

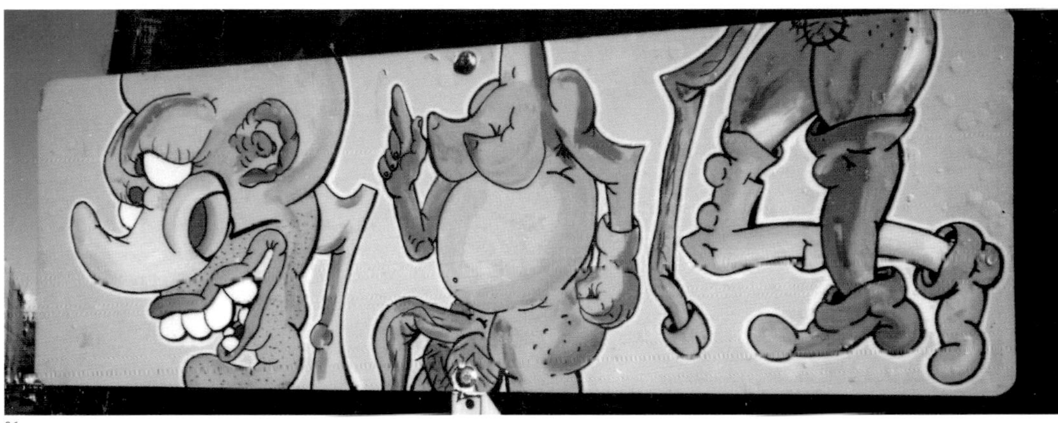
06

An interview with Buddy Lembeck

Name: Buddy Lembek **Age:** 26 **Hometown:** Born in Cincinnati, Ohio (USA), currently residing in Los Angeles, California (USA).

Cities to find your art:
Los Angeles, Cincinnati, New York, London, Brussels.

How did you come up with your character/style?
It mostly developed in math class during my junior year of high school. I was taking Algebra with a bunch of freshmen, and I was so bored and depressed in the class. I just kept drawing and doodling instead of taking notes, and I began forming organic noodle-like characters that eventually became the basis for most of my graffiti and street art imagery.

Do you have special message?
With each piece I create, the message will often change. It depends on variety of circumstances, such as the location where I'm installing it, current social or political situations, and, of course, what kind of mood I'm in.

How did you get into street art and why?
The street artist Darius Jones and I grew up in Cincinnati together, and we'd been friends since kindergarten. During high school, he was writing graffiti under the tag name "Verbs", and that's when he introduced me to the graffiti world. By the tail end of high school, I began making bus posters, wheat pasting, and bombing. I never used letterforms; I just applied the drawings in my sketchbooks to the surfaces on the street. I couldn't stop tagging, painting, and bolting my characters all over the place. I didn't really think I would be doing this for years; it was just addictive and I fell in love with the instant gratification, the adventures and the easy access to a large public audience.

Favorites street artists and why:
Darius & Downey, ESPO, Cost & Revs, Five, Leon Reid, Shepard Fairey, Keith Haring, Swoon, Twist–These artists are all originals at what they do, and they have all pushed the boundaries of what graffiti or street art is defined as in their time. They also all share a great work ethic that is inspiring enough in itself.

Other interests:
I'm just as much a filmmaker as I am a street artist. I recently finished a documentary about a group of graffiti writers entitled "NOBODYS", but most of my work usually consists of short comedy films and music videos (to see my films, visit www.blondchili.com).

Inspirations:
Poor advertising, pop culture, public access TV, middle America, people in general, and current events.

Do you have any stories related to street art?
From November 2000 to January 2001, myself and Darius Jones, along with a little help from another artist named Tadpole, began writing messages on train and highway overpasses along I-75 and I-71 in Cincinnati, OH with white bucket paint. The messages used local hero's names, former Cincinnati Reds players, pop culture icons, and classic religious messages. While a few of the messages were pure absurdity, such as "I PLAY YOGA", others dealt more with social commentary and funny observations. At the time it was a release for both of us to pursue such a crude raw project; it was funny, because it was about the ugliest thing we had done together, but it got the biggest reaction that we had had up until that time. Thousands of people saw them on the highways. Some people seemed to think they were pretty funny and others thought that they were offensive, as usual.
A local radio show began taking notice of the messages and mentioned them several times on the air. So Darius and I called the station and told them that we were the artists behind the messages.
We ended up talking for an hour and a half on a Republican, conservative talk radio show on 700 WLW about graffiti and what we were about. And, the DJ actually liked the content we were using. It was so bizarre and surprising.
While on the air, Darius and I were able to speak to the head of highway maintenance, a weatherman we wrote a message about, and Linda Haltertop (the leader of the anti graffiti "Keep Cincinnati Beautiful" task force). It was a great opportunity to talk to these people and share our views with them, but even after we made it clear that we were not in a gang or a threat to the public, Linda Haltertop still went on the news and tried to scare the public into believing we were a threat by giving the impression that we were in a gan, and that Darius Jones and I were in the KKK. It was ridiculous. While we were on the radio, a local FOX news channel got in touch with us and wanted to meet up for an interview. We made them meet us at a Chuck E. Cheese restaurant (a playland-themed kids pizzeria chain), but when we met up with the news team, the cameraman refused to shoot us with the Chuck E. Cheese sign in the background.
Other messages written on the overpasses during that period:
- CHRIS SABO DIED FOR OUR SINS (former Cincinnati Reds player)
- I VANDALISM
- KELLY WILL YOU DIVORCE ME
- I MADE OUT WITH MARGE SCHOTT (chain-smoking elderly woman and former owner of Cincinnati Reds)
- PAT BERRY SAT ON ME (overweight local weatherman)
- COLIN POWELL = VANILLA ICE
- LETS BE FRIENDS
- ROB DIBBLE BUSS ME UPSIDE THE HEAD (former Cincinnati Reds player with a bad temper)
- GIRLS FART, REALLY
etc.

The project lasted only a few months before things got out of hand and legal action followed. I won't delve into that, but we made it out okay in the end.

01 Latex paint and marker. Los Angeles, USA. Easter morning, 2004
02 Latex paint. Cincinnati, USA. 2000
03 Latex paint, spray paint, marker. Los Angeles, USA. 2005
04 Buddy Lembek dressed as a construction worker. New York, USA. 2003
05 "Colin Powell=Vanilla Ice" TV Screenshot. Cincinnati, USA. 2001
06 Spray paint & latex. New York, USA. 2002

OPT

Bordeaux, FR

01

OPT's big posters, which can be found in cities such as Berlin, Paris, Amsterdam, Pau, Prague, Barcelona, New York to name just a few, emerged through his love for the colors black and white. The 28-year-old started street art because he was sad and discouraged but writing on walls gave him a smile back, he says. When asked for some stories related to street art he just stated some words related to the street: "curious-fun-choice-city-dust-old-window-boring-stirring-rain-night-furious-winter-light-cold-walk-works-pavement-pedestrians-food-tramp-houses-overcrowded-dirty-stockage."

WWW.FOTOLOG.NET/OPT

02

03

04

01 Amsterdam, NL. 2005
02 Bordeaux, FR. 2005
03 Prague, CZ. 2005
04 Pau, FR. 2005

Dr.D

London, UK

01

02

02

Dr.D spent much of the late twentieth century researching a vaccination technique for global corporations, so that they might survive the Y2K virus. After years spent closeted in a small and dusty laboratory she was shocked to find, that in reality nothing happened other than share prices in information technology support companies rocketed and anti-viral software houses experienced their very own gold rushes. Dr.D has spent the last five years taking her revenge on the corporations, that led her down this ill fated path. Using cut and paste style, Dr.D is now working for you.

If you have a problem with a corporation, if nobody else will help you, and if you can find her, maybe you can hire Dr.D.

WWW.DRD.ORG.UK

03

04

04

T H E A R T O F R E B E L L I O N 2

An interview with Dr.D
Name: Dr.D **Hometown:** London, UK
Age: Never ask a woman her age, cheeky!

How did you start creating street art?
Started about 1999 to 2000 with the "SUDDENLY EVERYTHING SUCKS" Microsoft piece–a bit of an accidental attempt at modification really. Turned out no-one else was doing stuff quite like it.

Do you have any stories relating to street art?
It's all been quite uneventful...apart from falling off ladders, being chatted up by drunks in the middle of the night, and once dropping my brush and having it handed back to me by a cop who didn't realise what I was doing...

How do you prepare your artwork?
Each board is different. Sometimes you have two boards, that are the same and use letters cut out from one and teased back to a thin layer to re-stick (like the "I'M A BIT SHIT" board). Sometimes you have two different boards where you think part of one cut out and teased back so it re-stick will put a totally different slant on the other (like the "STARTS WARS", Darth Blair). In case you are wondering, the Blair face came from a political board by the Conservative Party. It was during an election, and it was just chance the boards were up at the same time. "YOU'RE JUST A GRASS WITH A BADGE" was made very simply with white on black letters done on a home computer and photocopied (so the ink won't run when it is wet). The "I AM WHAT I AM............CRAP"-Reebok conversion was done by tracking down the right typeface and having it cut out in vinyl sticky lettering by a sign maker's shop.

What is your message?
It's a shout back at the billboards which pollute every vista in London.
It's me shouting back at THE MAN, and maybe making like minded individuals feel like there is hope in this fucked up world.......

What is your favourite of the billboards you have modified??
Maybe the very first as it led to a whole lot more. I never planned on making a big name for myself and I still don't. It's just one board at a time. The first was "SUDDENLY EVERYTHING SUCKS", and an Australian website featured it after someone sent in a photo. A friend told me they'd seen it on there and then it appeared on the Guardian newspaper's website. What got me was the power of what I'd achieved totally unintentionally with the simplest of tools. I now had a release for my angry side.

How do people tend to react towards your artwork?
I've only ever had people taking photos or saying, well done' as they pass.
Most people don't notice me and that is essential to staying active and not getting sued/prosecuted.

Have you ever got into trouble with the Police when making your art?
For legal reasons I cannot really elaborate, but if you look like a criminal you will get arrested like one. The more brazen you are, the more chance you will get away with it.

01 Modified billboard of a fast food restaurant. London, UK. 2005
02 Modified billboard of a TV channel London, UK. 2005
03 Modified billboard of a sports shoe manufacturer. London, UK. 2005
04 Modified billboard of a bank. London, UK. 2005

GOMEZ BUENO

Los Angeles, USA

01

WWW.GOMEZBUENO.COM

02

03

04

05

THE ART OF REBELLION 2

01
Location: Mexico City. MEX. 2002
Comment: This billboard is in Mexico City. In the year 2002 I was invited to do a gallery show at La Panaderia, I spent a month and a half there. I got really busy and decorated several billboards until I got arrested. This is by far the biggest one, I had a crew of 6 people to install it.
Medium: Ink on paper

02, 05
Location: Santander, ES. 2003
Comment: I had a show at galeria Siboney. Right in front of the gallery they have these entrances to an underground parking. I decorated 3 of them.
Medium: Vinyl on glass

03
Location: Los Angeles, USA. 2004
Comment: This is one of many cars I have decorated, I started this project in 2004 and still today it's going strong. There are quite a few driving around the freeways of LA. But I also have done some cars in other cities.

04
Location: Mexico City, MEX. 2002
Comment: Another billboard from Mexico City. This one is acrylic on canvas and then installed to the billboard. The canvas had grommets and we used elastic cords to tight it up

Comments by Gomez Bueno. November, 2005

INKUNSTRUCTION

Niort, Metz, Valence, FR

01

Inkunstruction is a group of three artists – St Brece, Same and Pico. Located in three different cities they collaborate on exhibitions, art projects and as a design studio. Inkunstruction was the name of their first exhibition as a team and so they decided to keep it as the name of the group.
– INK KUNST CONSTRUCTION.

WWW.INKUNSTRUCTION.COM

02
03
04
05

01-05 Niort, Metz, Valence, FR. 2005

KMR

Bournemouth, UK

01

Based on the South Coast of England the work of KMR has been seeping onto the street in different forms for the last few years. His "eyes" project was started in 2004 and consist primarily of hand-painted wheat-pastes, as well as deviations onto cardboard and adhesive backed paper. They can be found in various towns and cities in both the UK and Europe. "To me they are purely a graphic – and it's all about the placement and the fact that they are just there... at one with the banal environment they find themselves in – a symbiotic relationship built on a foundation of stoic principles. I didn't want to humanise them or have them portray any kind of emotion, likewise they don't seek a conscious involvement from anyone who passes by them. While they last they are just content to be (and watch)."

WWW.FOTOLOG.COM/K_M_R

02

03

04

05

01 Poster. Barcelona, ES. 2004
02 Traffic sign. Poster. Bournemouth, UK. 2005
03 Poster. Bournemouth, UK. 2004
04 Poster. Barcelona, ES. 2004
05 Poster. Bournemouth, UK. 2005

MAMBO

Paris, FR

01

02

This little "free project" is just a logical following to what Mambo did before in India, Senegal, Italy, USA, Japan or around France. His goal is to travel in a different way, to use the art to meet people and to exchange emotions. The experience gets more and more satisfying to him as he is experiencing it now with his family as it brings more surprises in the human way, but also as he is becoming a better artist and a better photographer than before. All characters were hand painted on paper by brush, in Mambo's studio in Paris in July 2005 and pasted in Brazil's nordeste in August 2005.

03

04

05

01
Location: Aquiraz, BRA. 2005
Comment: Very cool little town. The city installed speakers in the streets playing music.

02
Location: Prainha, BRA. 2005
Comment: Ex military base, on the beach, which used to be a bombing field for planes in the 40's-50's.

03
Location: Fortaleza, BRA. 2005
Comment: In Fortaleza's old town, crowds of people, stores and restaurants. Very popular.

04
Location: Prainha, BRA. 2005
Comment: An empty house. A family lives on the back of it, and they loved the piece. The foto is taken from the village's football field

05
Location: Japao, BRA. 2005
Comment: The piece is inside the capoeira's school on the hill of Japao, a fisherman's village with a small favela on the hill. I practiced capoeira in France and i lived in brazil when I was a kid, so speaking their language, practicing fighting with them and offering paintings to the village (I also painted a fisherman's boat) made me get to know almost eveybody there and meet great friends, many parties in the house I rented, fires on the beach, playing instruments, singing and drinking fresh caipirinhas, eating fresh fish and seafruits. Reallife! "Mandinga Cearense" is the name of the local capoeira group, now brothers of my group in France, "Aguia Dourada".

Comments by Mambo. December 2005

SKEWVILLE

NewYork, USA

01

Skewville Laboratories was first founded by twins Ad and Droo after they quit their day jobs in the mid 90's. Their deviance dates back to the early eighties when they built secret clubhouses and custom sling shots to battle local bullies. Now and then they have combined their skills of graphics and engineering know-how to create the underground science that has been fueling and funding their deviant lifestyle.

Past Skewville legends have revealed tales of 16 ft. animated plywood snowmen, incognito smokable lunchboxes and silkscreen re-bootlegged t-shirts. Skewville has also been making great advancements in the experimentation of street stamping technology along with currently revamping city materials to communicate phrases like "FRESH" and "FAME GAME".

Yet, most known is Skewville's sneaker-mission "WHEN DOGS FLY". Since 1999 they have been manufacturing fake wooden sneakers, which can be found tossed over thousands of power lines in your neighborhood and all over the world. This global activity has spawned a "Skywarz" where other artisans now toss stuff up.

WWW.WHENDOGSFLY.COM

02

03

04

05

06

01
Location: Lower East Side, Elizabeth St. Projects. NYC, USA 2005
Comment: While taking this photo, some guy was hanging out the window watching us. We asked if he knew about the hanging sneakers and the myth that they ment drugs were sold here. He said "I never heard of that, why? you need some?"

02
Location: Skewville's Secret Lab 2005
Comment: We make a few new editions every year depending on the location and/or mission. If we fly, we always call the airline to find out exactly how much weight and baggage we can bring on the plane. Our last flight to London we brought only 2 pair of pants and over 200 pairs of Sneakers.

03
Location: Chinatown. NYC, USA 2005
Comment: Many vendors sell crap on the streets in chinatown. This tourist trap is where you get your bootleg Fendi bags and Gucci contraband. It seemed like the perfect place for fake hype.

04
Location: SOHO. NYC, USA 2005
Comment: Originally the wheels spun on this piece. Two weeks later, Just when you thought New York was safe again, someone stole the rims and smashed the headlights.

05
Location: SOHO. NYC, USA 2005
Comment: The infamous candle building in NYC is a street art mecca . Half the artists in this book have traveled far to pay homage and add to its many layers of fame. Unfortunatly, a lot of that art is peeled off or covered over on a weekly basis.
Being locals we knew we had to step up our game, so we bolted this piece to the building that says it all.

06
Location: Lower East Side. NYC, USA 2005
Comment: Mark and Sara from Wooster Collective had mentioned this piece on their annual street art walking tour. They later told us how funny it was that people were still asking where it was while standing right in front of it.

Comments by Skewville. January, 2006

EXHIBITIONS
ART SHOWS

01

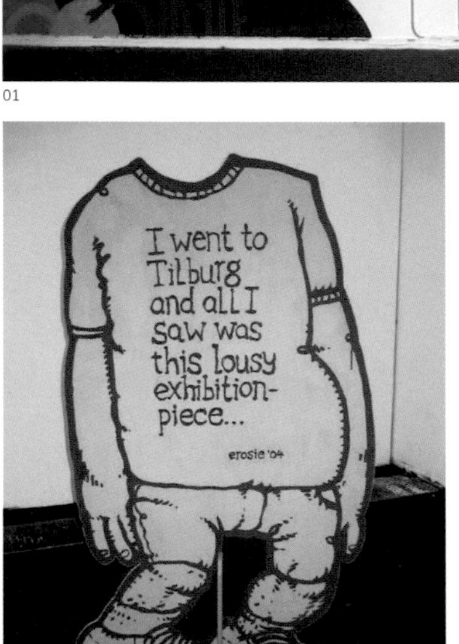

02

03

04

05

06

07

08

09

10

11

12

13

01 Street art battle GER vs NL. Artist: Frühstück. Tillburg, NL. 2004
02 Street art battle GER vs NL. Artist: Erosie (Eindhoven, NL). Tillburg, NL. 2004
03 Street art battle GER vs NL. Artist: BFree. Tillburg, NL. 2004
04 Artist: SFaustina. Transport Gallery, Los Angeles, USA. 2004
05 Customised sneaker. Artist: Tofer. Los Angeles, USA. 2004
06 Vinyl toy. Artist: MCA. USA. 2005
07 Artist: Sickboy. Bristol, UK . 2005
08 Artist: Gorb (Brighton, UK). Amsterdam, NL. 2005
09 Artist: Wood. Rotterdam, NL. 2004
10 Artist: Tofer. Los Angeles, USA. 2004
11 Artist: Tron, London, UK. 2005
12 Illustration for Fenchurch clothing. Artists: Kid Acne (Sheffield, UK). 2004
13 Sketchel bag. Artist: Jeremyville. Sidney, AU. 2004

URBAN EDGE SHOW

Milan, I

01

The Urban Edge was a show held in spring 2005 at P4, Milan. The exhibition showed works of the crème de la crème of urban art. Curators were Bo130, Microbo and Abner Price.
Artists (Action zone): 108 (I), 2501 (I), Abbominevole (I), Alexone (FR), A. Price & C. Tedeschi (USA), Akim & Idee (GER), Bo130 (I), Blu (I), Che Jen (USA), Doze Green (USA), Dr.Lakra (MEX), El tono & Nuria (ES), Galo (I), Influenza (NL), Jeremy Fish (USA), Kami & Sasu (JAP), Krudality crew (I), Kiku (USA), Microbo (I), Miss Van (FR), Mr Jago (UK), Nano 4814 (ES), Ozmo (I), Papik Rossi (I), Sharp (USA), Shepard Fairey (USA), Space 1026 (USA), Swoon (USA), Skwerm (USA), The London Police (NL), Will Barras (UK), Why style (I).
Artists (Photography): Adam Wallacavage, Alex Fakso, Cleph, Charlie Ahearns, Henry Chalfant, Lisa Kahane, Jamel Shabazz, Mirai Pulvirenti, Ricky Powell. Additionally various performances, BMX-/Skate-shows and a limited edition sneakers/toys exhibition were held.

02

03

04

05

06

07

08

01 Big wall (various artists) 2005
02 Artists: Shephard Fairy (Los Angeles, USA) vs. The London Police (Amsterdam, NL). 2005
03 Artist: Jeremy Fish (San Francisco, NL). 2005
04 Artist: Skwerm (USA), Galo (Amsterdam, NL), . 2005
05 Artist: Microbo (Milan, I), Bo130 (Milan, I). 2005
06 Artist: Shephard Fairy (Los Angeles, USA). 2005
07 Artist: Kami (Tokyo, JAP). 2005
08 Artist: Sasu (Tokyo, JAP). 2005

FINDERS KEEPERS

London (UK), Barcelona (E), Milan (I), Hamburg (GER)

01

02

03

04

05

06

07

08

Finders Keepers was formed in June 2003 after D*Face and PMH got talking in a dingy East London boozer. They both drunkenly agreed that the lack of action in London needed to be rectified and an event that could pull together all the artists with work up in the streets had to be a good thing. "Galleries weren't interested and didn't represent us, so we decided to hold an illegal gallery" D*Face said. "We had seen that Dave the Chimp had arranged a free street gallery of his work back in 2001, so we figured an event based only on found trash in the streets, without permission, had to be the way forward; it cost the artists nothing but their time this way". Two weeks after this initial drunken conversation, and with Mysterious Al joining the gang, they held their first Finders Keepers event on Friday 13th June 2003. The Chimp was signed up immediately after, and Finders Keepers Crew was formed. Since that time, FKC has held a number of these "Illegal Street Galleries" in London, Barcelona, and Milan, as well as organising exhibitions in bars in London and independent galleries in Hamburg and Barcelona, and turning a whole London Underground train into a gallery by replacing all the advertising with paintings. The street galleries always attract between 15 and 40 artists, and upward of 150 art lovers, desperate to get their hands on free paintings made on suitcases, bar stools, fridge doors and even the wings of dead pigeons.
– Dave the Chimp. January, 2006

09

10

13

11

12

14

15

16

01 PMH at work. FK Hamburg, GER. 2005
02 FK Barcelona, ES. 2004
03 1st. Finders Keepers. London, UK. 2003
04 Artist: Miss Van. FK Barcelona, ES. 2004
05 FK Barcelona, E. 2004
06 Artists: Bo 130, TLP, Freaklub. FK Barcelona, ES. 2004
07 Artist: Gamebombing. FK Barcelona, E. 2004
08 Artists: D*Face, Asbestos, Dist, TLP, PMH. FK Barcelona, ES. 2004
09 Artists: Tabas, Chimp. FK Barcelona, ES. 2004
10 Artist: KMR. FK Milan, I. 2005
11 Artist: Influenza, Chimp, KMR, TV Boy. FK Milan, I. 2005
12 Artist: Jace. FK Barcelona, ES. 2004
13 FK Barcelona, ES. 2004
14 Artist: Chimp. FK London, UK. 2004
15 Artists: Mysterious Al, Gorb. FK Barcelona, ES. 2004
16 Artist: Seomra. FK Barcelona, ES. 2004

FAVORITE FIENDS

Outside Institute. London, UK

01

The Outside Institute, a gallery in Paddington, West London was founded by like minded individuals who are directly or indirectly involved in this movement. The 2,000 square foot space has been designed to allow artists to exhibit their work in an easy-going, stylish environment, specifically showcasing those people embracing the urban environment as a creative medium, and promoting the urban art movement.

Following hotly on from the inaugural exhibition "Seen, the God father of graffiti", the Outside Institute brought together 30 of the UK's most innovative painters, illustrators, animators, sculptors and urban artists: Banksy, Pete Fowler, Shok1, Will Barras, Mr Jago, D*Face, Matt Sewell, Insa, Part 2, Gorb, Optic, Dist to name a few.

The Outside Institute divided up its walls with each artist being given free reign with a strip that runs floor to ceiling of the gallery, enabling each artist to express themselves freely: to hang canvases and or paint directly onto the walls, there were no limitations.
"A few of our favourite fiends" aimed to show the far reaching and influential impact directly or indirectly of graffiti art on so many artists in many diverse directions.

02

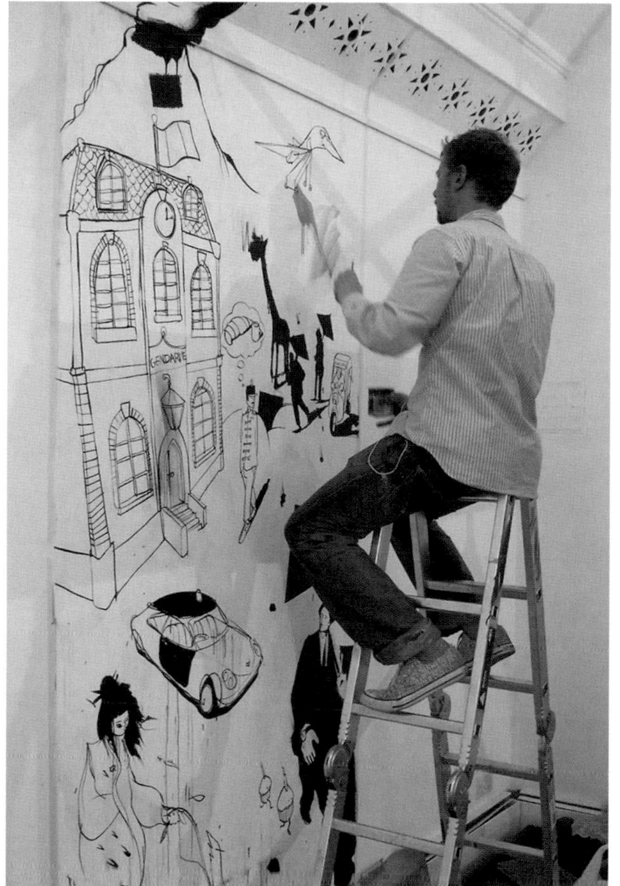
03

04

06

05

07

08

- **01** Exhibition main view. 2005
- **02** Flyer for the event. 2005
- **03** At work. Artist: Will Barras. 2005
- **04** At work. Artist: Mr. Jago. 2005
- **05** Peckham rock. Artist: Banksy. 2005
- **06** Turn up the silence. Artist: Conor Harrington. 2005
- **07** D*Pope. Artist: D*Face. 2005
- **08** Outside Institute beasts paw logo by D*face. 2005

VRS BACKSTAGEPASS

by Flying Fortress & Dave the Chimp.
London, UK

01

If you're going to call your crew VISUAL ROCK STARS you have to kick ass, and when the Outside Institute offered us our first show in London in their 2,000 square foot gallery we knew we had to kick ass hard! As Flying Fortress and myself live in different countries we decided the gallery would be our studio for the run of the show, so that we could work together and so the public could see the show grow, hence the title "Backstage Pass". I had the idea to construct a stage and cardboard instruments so that we could open the show with a "live" gig by our imaginary rock band "ViRuS". To add an extra rock starelement to the show we held various events including temporary tattoo days, a fashion shoot, toy signing, and a wet t-shirt competition, as well as spending some time out painting in the streets. On the opening night our friends PMH, Mysterious Al, and Ichi Bunny joined us on stage, all glam-rocked up, and all hell broke loose as ViRuS mimed it's way through half an hour of classic 80's hair metal like Aerosmith and Van Halen. Beer was thrown, guitars were smashed, and the crowd went crazy! "Backstage Pass" was a concept piece, and, with people still talking about the show six months later, I think it had the impact we hoped it would. And now I can't wait to see where people take this ,street' art form in a gallery setting next.

– Dave the Chimp, January 2006

02

03

04

05

06

07

08

09

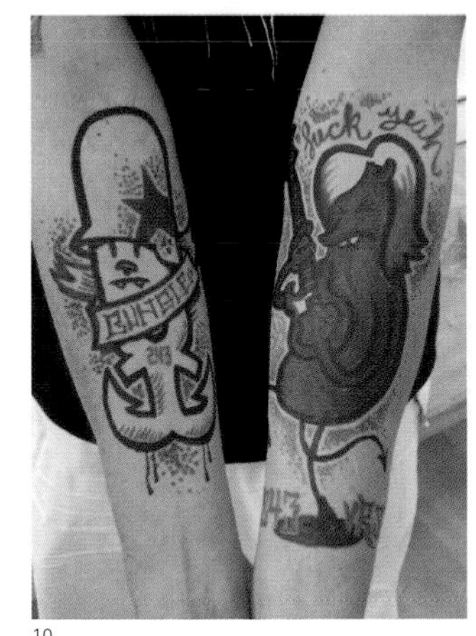

10

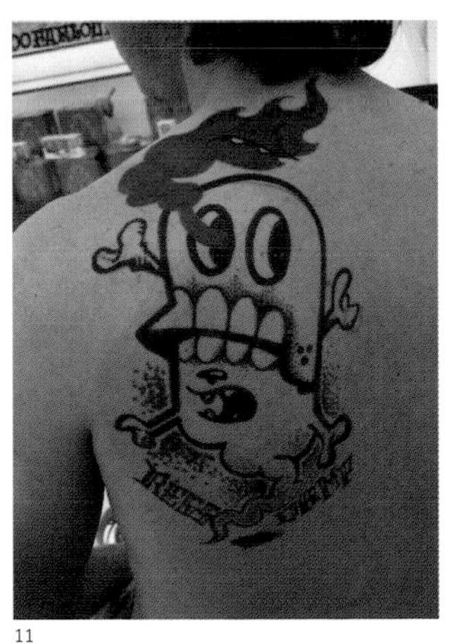

11

12

13

01 Exhibition main view. 2005
02 Tatoo. 2005
03 Tatoo Photo wall. 2005
04 The instruments. 2005
05 Chimp & Fortress sketch. 2005
06 Chimp & Fortress rooftop graffiti. 2005
07 Canvases. 2005
08 Wall. 2005
09 Canvas. 2005
10 Tatoo. 2005
11 Tatoo. 2005
12 Tatoo. 2005
13 ViRuS live. 2005

IKEART

Montpellier, FR

01

02

03

04

05

This show, a sarcastic reinterpretaion of the famous furniture house, was realised in March 2005 in Montpellier. The artists designed individial showrooms similar to the original IKEA houses but in their own style. Participating artist were: Koralie, Lola, Mkan, Supakitch, Starsky, MC 1984, GUM, EE and Des Trucs de Filles.

01 Children bedroom. Artist: Supakitch. 2005
02 Kitchen. Artist: MKan. 2005
03 Children bedroom. Artist: Supakitch. 2005
04 Garage. Artist: StArsky. 2005
05 Kitchen. Artist: MKan. 2005

THE DILLY
London, UK

01

02

03

04

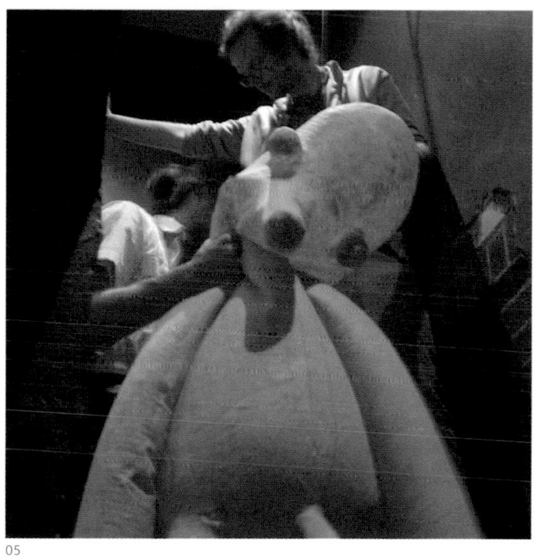
05

The Dilly show 01 featured stefan marx, bfree, NEW studios, Dave the chimp, Pinky, Paris Hair, the Mentary Brothers, Ichi the bunny and Kabe. It was at East London's Dreambagsjaguarshoes and held to launch the first issue of the dilly zine. Giant ducks in love. Graffitti apples. Rubber monsters. Mud Men. Knitting sheep and dizzee rascal I wanted to put on the kind of show that I felt wasn't being put on in London. A show featuring exciting artists doing exciting work. Artists that weren't overexposed, pompous or boring. A show put on for the art's sake, for the fun of hanging out and creating together, rather than to sell a product or satisfy a sponser. I was fed up of artists posting canvas works to shows and not doing anything fresh on site. I was fed up of the same stale mediums painted trainers/toys/ stale canvases on stale white walls. I was fed up of the same selection of artists that always gets chosen for group shows, often leaving out the more adventurous and sometimes better artists. I was fed up of the same boring artistsdoing just the same jpeg - image, and not pushing things in anyway. The reason for the show (and the zine) was to try and change things by doing it the way I wanted to do them, as no one else seemed to be doing it.

So I got a few of my personal favorite artists in Europe, who happened to be my friends and invited them down with only one goal: to do a show that will blow people away for good or bad. It worked.

– PMH. December, 2006

01 Dilly dolls. Artist: Bfree (Amsterdam. NL). 2005
02 Artist at work. Artist: Bfree (Amsterdam. NL). 2005
03 Artist: Paris Hair. 2005
04 The Dilly. 2005
05 Dilly doll. 2005

MONSTERS! BEWARE!

Bethnal Green. London, UK

01

31st October – Halloween – is my favourite celebration of the year (it's actually New Years Eve for Pagans). It's all about horror and ghosts and monsters, which I loved since I was a child, and it gives you an excuse to make things and dress up. In 2003, Finders Keepers Crew had an exhibition and party in a bar in East London, and in 2004 I celebrated by heading to the South Coast to hook up with some friends and poster the outside of the house once lived in by Mary Shelley (the author of "Frankenstein"). This year I decided to repeat my "Monsters! Beware!" exhibition from 2000, where I filled a park with cut-out cardboard monsters, but this time around I invited a bunch of friends to join me. I chose a wooded area in a park near my flat, partly because it's used by junkies to get high and I thought a little horror might wake them up to what they're doing to their bodies. Our motley crew gathered at my flat to finish our pieces, then headed commando style to the park at 2am. Product Two brought a life-sized cut-out wooden man whose legs would spin so he looked like he was running away, Saru constructed a 10 foot high skeleton, while Kabe made origami bats and ghosts. I built a number of life-size gravestones, papier mache zombie heads and arms, and assorted cut out monsters, and put together a whole graveyard scene. Once finished, we put up posters to advertise the exhibition in the local area, and went to Kabe's house for tea and reefer! Another successful Halloween! I can't wait 'til next year!
– Dave the Chimp. January 2006

02

03

04

05

06

07

01 Artist: Chimps Zombie Graveyard. 2005
02 Artist: Ichi Bunnys Monster Bunny Heads. 2005
03 Artist: Gorb creates a junkies dream world. 2005
04 Artist: KMRs evil rat-eating monsters. 2005
05 Artist: Mandy made many plush ghosts and monsters. 2005
06 Artist: Saru's giant skeleton. 2005
07 Chimps poster for the event. 2005

VINYL KILLERS

Organised by Klutch.
San Francisco, USA

01

02

03

04

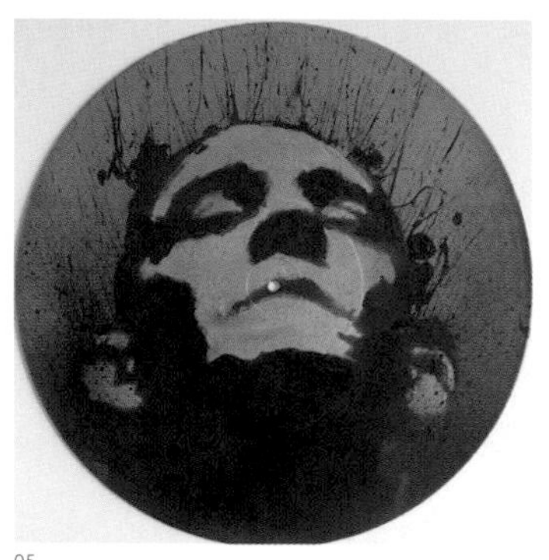
05

06

07

08

09

10

11

12

13

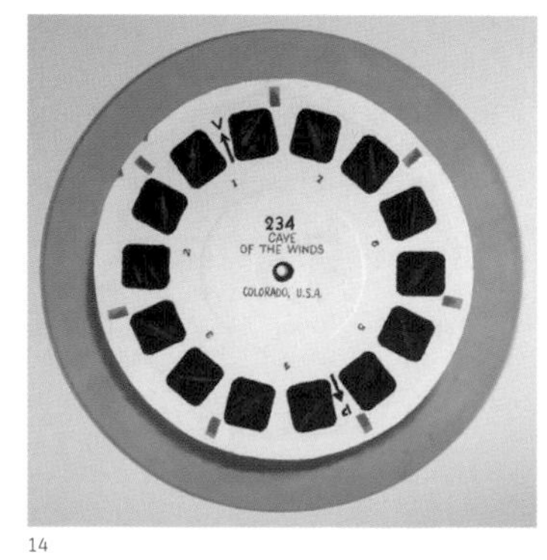

14

15

16

Vinyl Killers is a loosely based group of international artists who paint on old phonograph records and repurpose them as art. Founded in 2003 by Klutch there have been three annual exhibitions and vinyl work is now a staple of many street art exhibitions.
In 2005 the VK collective was invited to do an installation in the lobby at San Francisco's Hotel Des Arts and Klutch, the VK organizer, designed an entire room using his vinyl work and spray painted ornamentation that is a permanent installation at the hotel. As the medium of vinyl painting keeps growing Vinyl Killers has become it's annual gathering of the tribes.

WWW.VINYLKILLERS.COM

17

18

19

20

01 Artist: The Activist. 2005
02 Artist: Ripper 1331. 2005
03 Artist: Lord HAO. 2005
04 Artist: Torso Man. 2005
05 Artist: Sixten. 2005
06 Artist: The Activist. 2005
07 Artist: DL. 2005
08 Artist: DL. 2005
09 Artist: Urbanmedium. 2005
10 Artist: Ovaspray. 2005
11 Artist: Eelus. 2005
12 Artist: -struct. 2005
13 Artist: Ripper 1331. 2005
14 Artist: Mike Pearce. 2005
15 Artist: Ripper 1331. 2005
16 Artist: Mike Wargowski. 2005
17 Artist: Unknown. 2005
18 Artist: Unknown. 2005
19 Artist: Magmo the Destroyer. 2005
20 Exhibition overview. 2005

SECRET SANTA SWAP

Organised by Asbestos. Dublin, IRE

01

02

03

04

05

06

About two months before Christmas, I came up with the idea of organising artists from around the world, into a mammoth Secret Santa Swap. All they had to do, was to create a work of art and send it to another artist named on my list. In return, they'd get a piece of art from a completely different artist on the list. How simple is that? So, in essence, everyone created and received one work of art. I had no idea that so many artists would want to get involved, the final total was over 280 artists.

By mid November everyone had started creating and by early December most packages were on their way. Some took a lot longer than others to get to their destinations, but by December 25th most artists had an extra edition to the pile underneath their Christmas tree. A few lame bastards didn't send anything, and if they were on fire Santa wouldn't even piss on them. Their names were noted for being naughty, not nice and they were struck of the next year's line up.

Early in January I finally got around to putting all the images online. The variety and sheer quality of the work was astounding with artists like Swoon, D*Face, Chaz, JC Noria, C100, Bo130 & Microbo, Jet And Rubble, Calma, Thunder Cut, Yok, Faile, Eric Orr, Cum, Boris Hoppek, You Are Beautiful, Mjar & Galo, to name but a few, getting involved.

Before I decided to put the Secret Santa Swap together, I never realised so many people hated Christmas. So it was great to get dozens of mails from artists involved, thanking me for making their Christmas that little bit more bearable. One artist even wrote the following: ‚geeeeeeeeeez! i have never been so excited trying to open a Christmas present! your package is the best present somebody gave me since my chilhood when my parents gave me a bike! i feel really really in love with you guys! And have a good time this Christmas and i wish you next year to be better than 2004. PECE. ps: excuse my English.

See after months of hard graft to set this whole thing up, this one guy's happiness made it all worthwhile.

– Asbestos. January 2005

07

08

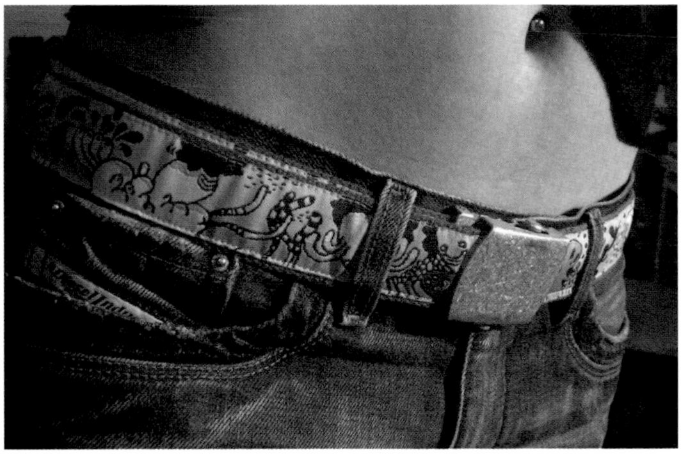

09

10

11

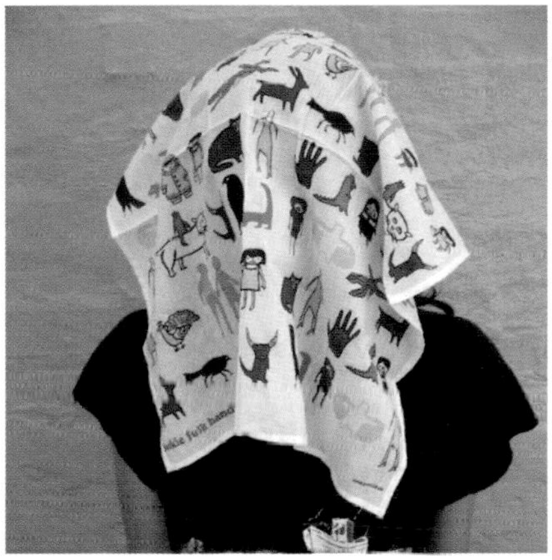

12

13

14

15

16

01 Secret Santa Swap logo.
02 Artist: 108, sent to: Derek Albeck.
03 Artist: Mike Clark, sent to: Liz Davison.
04 Artist: Swoon, sent to: Mjar.
05 Artist: Frühstück, sent to: Juan Carlos Noria.
06 Artist: Me Love, sent to: MDA.
07 Artist: Jon Burgerman, sent to: Faile.
08 Artist: Frühstück, sent to: Phonetic Control.
09 Artist: F. Iurilli, sent to: Thundercut.
10 Artist: Tchin, sent to: Asco.
11 Artist: Sml, sent to: Rep1.
12 Artist: T.Astonbooth, sent to: Mini Graff.
13 Artist: Thundercut, sent to: G.
14 Artist: Asbestos, sent to: Pece.
15 Artist: Cke, sent to: Robot Love.
16 Artist: Mjar, sent to: Toyesm.

FAILE

Shows in Zürich, San Francisco, New York, Los Angeles

01

02

03

04

05

06

07

08

09

01-04
Location: Les Complices Garelly in Zurich, CH. 2004
Medium: House paint, spray paint and stencil.
Comment: These 4 pieces are painted on the wall of Les Complices Garelly in Zurich. They were part of a street art festival, and since this festival was funded by the Swiss government, we were not able to sell any of the pieces even though it was a gallery show. So we decided to paint directly on the wall with those beautiful golden flames. Everyone dug it, but no one could take them back home. The show was up for a couple of weeks, then all of them were painted over. Such an ephemeral piece.

05-06
Location: New York, USA. 2004

07-08
Location: Los Angeles, USA. 2004

09
Location: New York, USA. 2004

Comments by Aiko. December, 2005

POLITICAL MINDED
by Heavyweight. Montreal, CAN

01

Heavyweight (HVW8) are an art, illustration and painting collective with studio based in Montreal and now more recently in Los Angeles. The collective is made up of Gene Pendon, Tyler Gibney and Dan Buller. The members come from backgrounds in comics, flyers, graffiti, design, painting and illustration. As live painters, the trio has toured through out Canada, the US as well as Europe, Puerto Rico and Japan, collaborating together to create live painting combined with DJ events, art installations and exhibitions. HVW8 has also released a music compilation, "Music as my Art" featuring collaborating music producers as well as the HVW8 t-shirt line.

WWW.HVW8.COM

02

03

04

05

Political Minded
Location: Montreal (CAN), New York & Los Angeles (USA), 2005
Comment: This work was the first full room mural installations as part of HVW8's "Political Minded" series. The idea was a collective commentary about war and the awareness of the political ideas and figures that struggle against it. The work was created in Montreal, 2004. Later the same installation was presented in New York in a shop in Lower East Side that was about to be demolished, and then in an art space in Los Angeles that was up for a month duration in 2005. As a departure from the past HVW8 subject matter of music and cultural icons portrayed in paintings created live from past music shows and festivals, the Political Minded series approached the theme of political icons and figures, and commentary through graphic design. Through portrait, the work features selected writers, and activists and statesmen whose work reveal ideas that they found moving and interesting to consider for our times: General Romeo Dallaire, Fela Kuti, Noam Chomsky, Shirin Ebadi, Paul Krugman and others. The murals shown in the pictures were done with latex.

Comments by HVW8. January, 2006

01-05 Political Minded. Montreal (CAN), New York, Los Angeles (USA). 2005

WK INTERACT

London, UK.

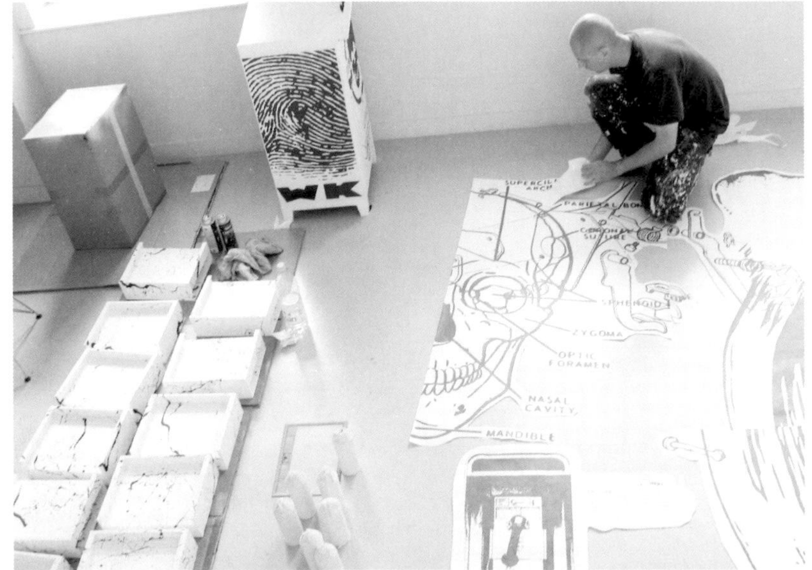
01

02

03

04

T H E A R T O F R E B E L L I O N 2

01-04
WK Interact
Location: Dpmhi store. London, UK. 2005
Comment: This show was at Maharishi's Dpmhi-store in Soho, London.

MAISON VERTE

by Russell Maurice. London, UK

01

02

03

04

01-04
Maison Verte
Location: Maharishi Churchill Gallery. London, UK. 2004
Comment: Maison Verte was Maurice's first UK exhibit. The show was composed of canvas works in various shapes and sizes, and installations of painted cardboard boxes, juice cartons, foam packaging, wood and geometric lamps.
Born in 1975 in Newcastle, Maurice has been involved in graffiti culture since the age of 12, which has been a major stylistic influence on his painting and design. Maurice's interest in nature - its energy, growth patterns, diversity, and cycles–has been an underlying theme in much of his work, obviously coupled with the heavy environmental issues that concern the modern world as a whole.
In particular, Maurice has revisited the idea of nature taking over the city and man-made items including in his work that has occasionally appeared on the streets of London in various formats such as brush painting, pen, bill posters and a few stickers. This idea is also shown with the usage of consumer waste materials as a way of drawing attention to our throw-away society.
Other themes suggest theoretical answers to the problems faced by the modern world such as biodegradable technology and clean energy harnessed from nature.

INPUT

IZASTICKUP (book)
Project, art direction and design by:
Bo130, microbo, The Don

Our generation grew up with all kinds of picture-cards and stickers. From the seventies onwards stickers have entered every household, first by collecting albums with cartoons', TV and football sets' picture-cards, then as advertising means for sportswear and casualwear brands, and now as an individual and artistic propaganda. It is exactly this last phenomenon that IZASTIKUP book focuses on: to indicate that times keep on changing and that the media adapt themselves to people's needs. As a matter of fact, stickers have now become part of our homes and have also gone out in the streets worldwide. Stickers come in any shapes and forms thanks to new technologies and to the Internet that is about to turn the world upside down by shortening the distances. It is incredible how much one can do and what results one can achieve with a few inches of adhesive paper.

IZASTIKUP, in fact, is a precious and unique collection of stickers coming from all over the world. The book shows more than 600 international artists, from totally different backgrounds.
In fact we have chosen to show to the pubblic as many stickers as possible and to give them the chance to take a closer look at each one of these mini jewels of spontaneous creativity by displaying, in a single volume, the variety of chosen signs, techniques within a multicolour and multiform jungle of styles and messages, things you may often find in the streets and sometimes pinned on your friend's fridge or on a friend of a friend's fridge or...

IZASTIKUP was also devised as an exact reproduction of a sketch book with the intention of sharing a fetish with the public at large that is normally the prerogative of artists and collectors.
The most amusing part of this project has been that of manually creating every single page, by posting stickers one by one – which reminded us of when we were kids.

We have chosen to include everybody without censoring or refusing to publish anybody, exactly because the main objective of this book was that of proving the phenomenon by documents but not that of defining an unstoppable artistic phenomenon born in the streets, as it would not stand any space or time limits. Never stop. Keep on sticking!
– Bo130, microbo, The Don. January, 2006.

Beautiful/Decay (magazine)

Founded on the theory that "if you can't find it, you make it", Beautiful/Decay was created to bridge the gap between art and graffiti, underground and mainstream, design and fine art, punk rock and hip hop, illustration and design, and most importantly high and low art. With a focus on cutting edge work in all the aforementioned genres, Beautiful/Decay strives to showcase new and emerging artwork whether it be interior or exterior.

Stencilrevolution (website)

Stencilrevolution is the largest stencil artist resource on the web containing stencil galleries, tutorials, forums, fonts, shop, artist profiles, EPS stencil downloads and much more. The well designed website is the main source for anyone interested in stencils.

Other Websites:
www.ekosystem.org
www.woostercollective.com
www.adbusters.org
www.designiskinky.net
www.mumia.org
www.amnestyusa.org

01

NICE TRY, BUT WE CAN'T BE STOPPED. SEE YOU...

PUBLISHING PROGRAMM

MONTANA WRITERTEAM
graffiti at its best
07.2006
ISBN 3-980-9909-5-8
ruedione
hardcover. 21cm x 29cm. 160 pages

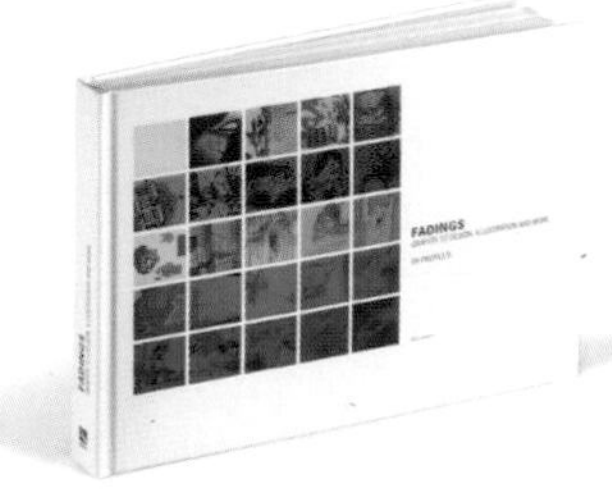

FADINGS
graffiti to design, illustration and more.
05.2005
ISBN 3-980-9909-0-7
s. schlee
hardcover. 28cm x 21cm. 240 pages

BEST OF STYLEFILE
the finest trains, walls, styles and interviews
of stylefile's first ten issues
07.2005
ISBN 3-980-9909-2-3
paperback. 23cm x 17cm. 256 pages

THE ART OF REBELLION
street art from all over the world
05.2005
ISBN 3-980-9909-1-5
c100
paperback. 16cm x 23cm. 144 pages

STYLEFILE.BLACKBOOK.SESSIONS.#01
graffiti on paper. scribbles, outlines and
full-colour-stuff
08.2002
ISBN 3-980-7478-2-4
m. christl
paperback. 23cm x 16cm. 160 pages

STYLEFILE.BLACKBOOK.SESSIONS.#02
graffiti on paper. scribbles, outlines and
full-colour-stuff
04.2004
ISBN 3-980-7478-8-3
m. christl
paperback. 23cm x 16cm. 160 pages

STRAIGHT LINES
ecb reso | a ten year graffiti-art dialog
04.2004
ISBN 3-980-7478-5-9
p. jungfleisch, h. beikirch
hardcover. 22cm x 15cm. 128 pages

HAMBURGCITYGRAFFITI
all about graffiti in hamburg. germany
10.2003
ISBN 3-980-7478-6-7
typeholics
hardcover. 21cm x 27cm. 176 pages

STYLEFILE
graffiti magazine
out every march, july and november
documenting in high quality the graffiti and
street art movement all over the planet
for details and further information check
http://www.stylefile.de